Praise for *Going Over Home*

"This book isn't just the story of one person's lifelong fight for justice for family farmers and rural communities. *Going Over Home* is a call that inspires the reader to stand shoulder to shoulder with family farmers in their daily struggle. It puts into words why all of us at Farm Aid believe in family farmers and rural America, and why their survival matters to all of us—no matter where we live."

—**Willie Nelson**, president, Farm Aid

"*Going Over Home* bears eloquent witness to Charlie Thompson's path toward a homegrown revolution of the heart, first illuminated by listening to many voices, then achieved by acting in solidarity with those who struggle for equality and inclusion along the wailing walls that America is building between itself and its own heart. Thompson's exemplary memoir confronts our separate and unequal pasts and gives us a heartfelt but clear-eyed narrative of American agricultural life and a bridge toward wholeness in a broken time."

—**Rev. Dr. William J. Barber, II**, codirector of the Poor People's Campaign; coauthor of *The Third Reconstruction*

"Told through moving stories of kinship and solidarity, *Going Over Home* brings much needed dimension and heart to our conversations about rural life and shows the strength of our bonds when love of place is animated by justice."

—**Elizabeth Catte**, author of *What You Are Getting Wrong About Appalachia*

"Charles D. Thompson, Jr.'s memoir isn't just a personal snapshot of some of the most important North American agrarian movements and thinkers. It's the history of a grateful rural educator's education written with a deep mix of generosity, curiosity, and wit, and it deserves to be read widely."

—**Raj Patel**, author of *Stuffed and Starved*

Also by Charles D. Thompson, Jr.

BOOKS

Maya Identities and the Violence of Place
The Human Cost of Food (editor, with Melinda F. Wiggins)
Indigenous Diasporas and Dislocations (editor, with Graham Harvey)
The Old German Baptist Brethren
Spirits of Just Men
Border Odyssey

DOCUMENTARY FILMS

The Guestworker (with Cynthia Hill)
Brother Towns (with Michael Davey)
We Shall Not Be Moved (with Chris Potter)
Faces of Time
Border Crossing 101
Homeplace Under Fire

Going Over Home

A SEARCH FOR RURAL JUSTICE
IN AN UNSETTLED LAND

Charles D. Thompson, Jr.

CHELSEA GREEN PUBLISHING
White River Junction, Vermont
London, UK

Photographs on pages 8, 20, 58, and 192 copyright © 2019 by Charles D. Thompson, Jr.

Photographs on pages 30, 42, 80, 88, 100, 114, 120, 142, 152, 174, 182, and 212 copyright © 2019 by Rob Amberg.

Cover photograph by iStock/Shauni.

Project Manager: Alexander Bullett
Acquisitions Editor: Benjamin Watson
Editor: Michael Metivier
Copy Editor: Diane Durrett
Proofreader: Laura Jorstad
Indexer: Linda Hallinger
Designer: Melissa Jacobson

Printed in Canada.
First printing September 2019.
10 9 8 7 6 5 4 3 2 1   19 20 21 22 23

Our Commitment to Green Publishing
Chelsea Green sees publishing as a tool for cultural change and ecological stewardship. We strive to align our book manufacturing practices with our editorial mission and to reduce the impact of our business enterprise in the environment. We print our books and catalogs on chlorine-free recycled paper, using vegetable-based inks whenever possible. This book may cost slightly more because it was printed on paper that contains recycled fiber, and we hope you'll agree that it's worth it. *Going Over Home* was printed on paper supplied by Marquis that is made of recycled materials and other controlled sources.

Library of Congress Cataloging-in-Publication Data
Names: Thompson, Charles D., Jr. (Charles Dillard), 1956- author.
Title: Going over home : a search for rural justice in an unsettled land / Charles D. Thompson, Jr.
Description: White River Junction, Vermont : Chelsea Green Publishing, [2019] | Includes index.
Identifiers: LCCN 2019012175| ISBN 9781603589123 (paperback) | ISBN 9781603589130 (ebook)
Subjects: LCSH: Farmers—Virginia—Biography. | Family farms—Management—United
    States—History.
Classification: LCC S417.T465 A3 2019 | DDC 338.109755--dc23
LC record available at https://lccn.loc.gov/2019012175

Chelsea Green Publishing
85 North Main Street, Suite 120
White River Junction, VT 05001
(802) 295-6300
www.chelseagreen.com

FOR HOPE.

We must learn to reawaken and to keep our-
selves awake, not by mechanical aids, but by
an infinite expectation of the dawn . . .

—HENRY DAVID THOREAU,
Walden, 1854

I'll be . . . wherever you look. Wherever they's
a fight so hungry people can eat . . . An' when
our folks eat the stuff they raise, an' live in the
houses they build—why, I'll be there.

—TOM JOAD, in John Steinbeck's
The Grapes of Wrath, 1939

In this universe we are given two gifts: the
ability to love and the ability to ask questions.

—MARY OLIVER, *Upstream,* 2016

CONTENTS

UNITED STATES DEPARTMENT OF AGRICULTURE
FARMERS HOME ADMINISTRATION
P.O. Box 147, Pittsboro, NC 27312
October 27, 1983

Mr. Charlie D. Thompson, Jr.
P.O. Box 1192
Pittsboro, NC 27312

Dear Mr. Thompson:

After careful consideration, we:

(XX) were unable to take favorable action on your application/request for Farmers
Home Administration services.
( ) are canceling/reducing the assistance you are presently receiving.

The specific reasons for our decision are:
1. Not considered a typical farmer in area,
2. Lacks practicle experience necessary to operate a farming operation
to insure reasonable chance of success.

If you have any questions concerning the decision or the facts used in making
decision and desire further explanation, you may request a meeting within 15 ca
days of the date of this letter. You may present new information or evidence
with possible alternatives for our consideration. You may also bring a represe
tive (or legal counsel) with you. Should we be unable to satisfactorily resolv
case, you will be advised of your appeal rights and how to begin the appeal pro
If, without good cause, you fail to schedule or attend this meeting, there will
no further appeal.

Photograph by Bonnie Campbell.

Opening | *1983*

*T*he envelope appeared too thin to hold more than a single page of paper. Was that already an indication? Marked for official use only by the US Department of Agriculture, I knew the letter inside contained the answer I had been eagerly awaiting—and also dreading—for nearly a month. My stomach clenched as I debated how I should open and read it. Should I wait for my fiancée, Hope, to get home? Should I sit down inside and read it alone? Or should I rip it open at the mailbox and get it over with?

Two months earlier, as instructed by the Farmers Home Administration (FmHA) loan officer, I went to two local banks to ask for money to buy land. Both dismissed my loan application out of hand. I didn't have to wait; at both banks I received just a quick, "Sorry, we don't make farm loans." Anticipating this response, I asked them to put their decisions in writing on bank stationery, as FmHA rules required proof of two rejections from private lenders before the government could consider me a candidate to apply to the FmHA. I would then be able to meet with a loan officer and demonstrate why I was a deserving candidate for a Limited Resource and Beginning Farmer Loan. Along with proof of ability to make payments, I needed a written farm plan, a letter indicating that I had an option on a piece of land, and proof of adequate preparation for the venture. I had completed all of that and left their office a month before with my file complete. The second big step was now up to FmHA: eligibility.

Established during the Great Depression, when banks were failing as fast as farms, FmHA's predecessor, the Rural Resettlement

1

Administration, was the brainchild of Franklin D. Roosevelt's newly formed USDA. That the agency's very name included the word *Resettlement* promised a New Deal for rural people. Its first director, Rex Tugwell, a progressive leader of his day, believed his job at the agency was, above all, to help the landless, sharecroppers in particular, buy land for the first time. There were special provisions for farmers of color as well as whites. "Beginning farmer" loans were a central component. The program was as close to a land reform effort as the United States ever came. Though the agency's name eventually changed—and agriculture itself transformed dramatically by the time I applied half a century later—its stated purpose evoked the same spirit. Their brochure, titled *This Is FmHA*, avowed their mandate to "help assure that the marginal farmer still has a chance to succeed on the land, and that rural young people can get a start in farming."

I studied the FmHA rules diligently. But the other half of the story is that during the two years prior, I had worked for an advocacy organization called the Rural Advancement Fund (RAF), spending long hours helping other farmers fight against farm foreclosures by the FmHA. I had answered calls on a hotline from farm families having loan problems. I had written a simple guide for farmers who were struggling to make their payments. I had met with hundreds of farmers who were desperate enough to admit in public they were about to lose their land. I knew that despite FmHA's mandate to take chances where banks could not, they were instead turning against family farmers. In their words, the agency's "work . . . involved taking risks," and those risks had "paid off in a stronger family-based agricultural system," but now the agency known as the "lender of last resort" was turning against the very farmers they were supposed to help. Thousands of government foreclosures were looming. Standing alongside farmers—Black, Native American, and white, many of them women—I had tried to stop the FmHA's massive sweep of farmers off their land and out of rural communities all across the nation. Some agricultural leaders said the demise of the small farmer was an inevitable part of the "progression" of capitalism, that the small farms would give way to larger and presumably more efficient farms.

Many, including family farmers I had worked with, disagreed. Our side believed that local farms were the backbone of many rural communities and that they had to be saved. Having many farmers care for our food system was much preferable to turning our sustenance over to corporations. We believed a fight for the very essence of agriculture was under way. Fighting this fight had been my full-time job.

In the midst of this work, and during the worst farm crisis since the Great Depression, it might sound strange or suspicious that I chose to apply for a loan. But this was no ploy; I was passionate about farming, and I had done everything I could to qualify. At the same time, I couldn't deny that my personal act, as inspired as it was by an innate drive to grow things, was also distinctly political. I was applying for myself, but also on behalf of others in the future. I had prepared and submitted a strong application that reflected some of my most heartfelt dreams, and couched within it were my beliefs about our agricultural system writ large. Yet, as I handed my packet to the loan officer, I knew my chances were slim; that everything I believed in both as a farmer and as an advocate would be put to the test. The envelope I now held in my hands was their response.

A major stumbling block in front of every farmer who applied to the FmHA was achieving eligibility, a status determined by a local, nonelected County Committee. In Chatham County, North Carolina, where I was attempting to apply, two older men had been appointed by the agency to make all of the eligibility decisions. In other words, only two men decided who could apply for government money in our county. Both were white. One of them was a forester and the other a semiretired corn and soybean farmer. My farm plan was to grow organic fruits and vegetables and organic eggs and meats, which the two men likely had no experience with or interest in. These men were large landowners. I only wanted to buy twenty-two acres. They were members of the old guard of the county. I was a relative newcomer, and a farm advocate. How much would my advocacy work factor into their decision?

I assumed the agency at large already had me in their sights. If the committee members had not previously known about me, I suspected the FmHA officer, getting word from Raleigh (in Wake County, just east of Chatham County), would have told them. Also, I'd heard of many cases where a County Committee had favored the powerful and discriminated against the smallest farmers, especially people of color, as small farmers were said to be inefficient and, therefore, in their minds, expendable. On paper, eligibility for beginning farmers was said to be based on objective criteria, which meant the two-man committee should decide solely on whether I had adequate knowledge of the type of farming proposed, and whether my farm plan could work financially. The premise was that they were to look over every farm plan on its own merits without deciding whether they approved of the individual. This was official government business after all, and the County Committee's job was to help determine suitability for the loan and perceived repayment ability of the proposed farm, not to judge or discriminate against the person applying.

In a perfect world, my line of work would not factor into their decision. The agency's organizational structure made it impossible for loan officers to know everyone in the county, and thus the committee, serving as representatives of the government, would help decide who was best suited to receive government money. But of course, this is not a perfect world. The result of this structure in the real world was to empower two or three men to make decisions about many other people's livelihoods, in rural counties where prejudices had become entrenched. Small groups of power brokers often have strong biases and wield their influence to suit their idea of how a farm community should look. The Rural Advancement Fund accumulated evidence of these kinds of committee prejudices. As I was applying for my loan, I had already helped African American and Lumbee farmers document and argue in appeal hearings how they had been shut out of the loan process. We saw evidence of racism, and there was talk of a class action lawsuit.

To be fair, I had not met those two gentlemen of the Chatham County committee face-to-face. Had we talked, I thought, maybe they would have been open-minded. Or maybe my advocacy work would make the agency skittish about doing something untoward, and they could be afraid I might use this in court. Maybe the two men didn't yet know about my activism, since they lived on the other side of the county. The acting loan officer who presented my case to them had worked in the county only for a few months, and she told me, "This is the best farm plan I've ever seen." Maybe she was too new at her job to know of my advocacy work; if she conveyed her confidence in my plan to the County Committee members, maybe there was a better chance they would review my proposal on its merits alone. After all, wouldn't they want me as a success story they could point to in the press?

All my hopes and doubts felt like electricity in my fingertips as I turned the letter over in my hand. I couldn't wait any longer. I tore a section of the flap, inserted my index finger and ran it down the side of the envelope, slid the letter out, unfolded it, and began to read. The single page was printed on letterhead and signed by Margo Burnette for Barbara Hinton, acting county supervisor of the FmHA:

> Dear Mr. Thompson,
>
> After careful consideration, we were unable to take favorable action on your application/request for Farmers Home Administration services.
>
> The specific reasons for our decision are:
> 1. Not considered a typical farmer in area,
> 2. Lacks practicle [sic] experience necessary to operate a farming operation to insure reasonable chance of success.

The letter continued with boilerplate language stating that I had the right to request further clarification, take legal counsel with me, and even submit new information for consideration. Then this: "Should we be unable to satisfactorily resolve your case, you will be advised of your appeal rights and how to begin your appeal process."

I immediately went back to my files and read over the eight-page marketing plan I had submitted for the Thompson Berry Farm. I opened a beer and sipped it as I reread everything, trying to uncover any problems with my case. I still believed I'd done everything right. Plus, I knew from our RAF hotline calls that the "typical farmer in area" was suffering. Bankruptcies and foreclosures among the "typical" farmers were rampant. We were in the midst of the American Farm Crisis that was being covered by news media all over the country. I was definitely atypical for the area, but wasn't that a good thing if the typical farms were failing? And I had worked hard to be a farmer all my life, including closely working alongside my farmer relatives. And didn't my master's degree in agricultural education count? I had been in charge of the gardens at an organic demonstration farm. I had met with Cooperative Extension Agents who helped me with my plan. I had consulted with other small-scale growers already in business in North Carolina. How much more experience and preparation can a beginning farmer have and still be called a beginner? If I had farmed with my parents, wouldn't I already have a chance to inherit land? Who were these loans for if not for someone like me?

An hour after I opened the envelope and read the committee's decision, Hope walked into the house. "I'm ineligible," I blurted out before she even put down her purse.

"What?!" Because we were not yet married, the FmHA rules said I had to apply alone. She, too, had worked as an advocate on our hotline we operated through the Rural Advancement Fund. She was the first staff member trained in Nebraska by the Center for Rural Affairs to take the responsibility of answering calls. And she knew my whole story better than anyone. "You have to appeal," she said.

She was right. Every fiber of my being said I had to fight this decision—not just for me, but for all small farmers. The next day, I would call the FmHA office and schedule the appointment, and follow their every instruction. I refused to lose, especially on a technicality. I knew I had a good case. But before the upcoming meeting, I would have much preparation to do. I needed more letters of recommendation from people who could speak about my farm experience. I would have to spend hours working through my story. I would have to study FmHA's regulations again. I was already

6

convinced I qualified; I just had to prove it to an agency determined to rid its rolls of small farmers. The FmHA had become a foreclosure machine. But that machine had not stopped me believing in our quixotic cause before, and I wouldn't let it now.

But for a night, I needed to pause and pine a little because the rejection was truly a loss for me. I knew my chances in a state-level appeal—where I had gone toe-to-toe with some of FmHA's most powerful players and lost—were slim. Anonymity, even if I'd squeaked by the committee as a random citizen, would be impossible going forward. Now the state officials would fight me both as an applicant and as an advocate, as they had all the other small farmers I had championed, and probably harder because I had been a thorn in their side. They had no right to discriminate against me; the loan I was applying for was US taxpayer money after all. But that reasoning had never stopped them from using such tactics before. I could name dozens of qualified farmers who had been either denied or cut off by FmHA. Why would I presume my case would be any different? But every farm dream begins with optimism. Every farmer must believe in the impossible in order to plant the first seed.

At the same time, I hated the whole agency. They acted against everything I had ever believed in and worked for, even the principles their own literature proclaimed. I wanted to retaliate, even though I knew anger wouldn't help. I had lost my temper once in an appeal hearing on behalf of a gentle, elderly couple whose hog farm was in foreclosure, and ended up apologizing to the farmers. I had lost my temper in part because I detested seeing them at the mercy of bureaucrats who seemed trained to be callous. Yet I had also learned in the process that arguing a case on emotion, or even based on my passionate idea of fairness, got me nowhere. I had to think strategically. I had to beat them at their own game. .

But that fight would have to wait. I set aside the FmHA files and walked outside to our little garden beside our house to pick lettuce and spinach for a salad for supper, and to breathe. Kneeling down in the grass beside our raised beds, with my stainless steel bowl at my knees, my thoughts turned to every farm I'd ever loved.

The author, Charlie Thompson, with his cousin Bruce Martin on their grandparents' farm.

Rooting | *1959*

*M*y earliest memory—from when I was barely three years old—took place on a farm. When no one was watching, I turned the backdoor handle, pushed open the wooden screen door, and ventured down the concrete steps to explore Grandma Jamison's fenced backyard. As I reached the bottom step, I let go of the door, which slammed behind me with a bang. Suddenly, a huge Rhode Island Red rooster, with its fleshy, blood-red comb flopping over one eye, came charging at me, chest bulging, neck feathers flared, wings arched, his orange eyes leveled on mine. As he bore down, the whole flock screeched in unison. I froze. I'm sure I screamed, too.

Just then the screen door burst open behind me, and my great-grandmother—eighty-two years old and wearing a dark dress and her long gray hair in a bun—grabbed my arm and pulled me behind her. She flung her other arm up to shoo the rooster away and yelled, "You get back there!" He made an immediate about-face and trotted back to the flock, shaking his feathers as if he had accomplished something. I nestled close to my great-grandmother's dress as she walked me back up the steps and into the house.

That is my only recollection of my mother's paternal grandmother, who was born in 1877. But it is the first of countless memories I retain of my rural relatives, their animals, and their farms in the Virginia Blue Ridge. Thankfully, I never stopped venturing outside, even when visiting my farming relatives for only an hour, even in dress-up clothes. Every turn of a door handle meant new adventures and lessons learned. Those forays are how I first came to embrace my sense of belonging to agriculture, and how I knew that I, too, wanted to be a farmer.

Once my family members found me at my grandpa Thompson's barn standing inside a circle of cattle towering over me and sniffing the little child among them. My family told me later that when the adults saw me near the barn they could only watch from a distance for fear the cows would trample me if they moved closer. So they waited as I communed with the cattle, and looked on until the cows lost interest and walked off, their calves trotting along behind them. Through my child's understanding, the cows did not see me as a threat, but instead seemed to speak with their eyes, lowering their enormous wet noses so close to mine that I could smell the grassy scent of their breath. As they edged their huge hooves toward me, careful not to step on my feet, I leaned toward them and sniffed them back, my hands remaining at my sides. Such moments, recounted through my family's storytelling as we gathered around Grandma's dinner table, grounded me, giving me a sense of belonging—in terms of both place and vocation—that stays with me to this day. Yet those memories always contained a touch of melancholy, because the places where I learned farming were already vanishing by the time I came to know them.

I remember never feeling we had stayed long enough; no matter how many times Grandma repeated her refrain before we left, "Stay and eat supper with us," I knew the answer always would be "No, we've got to get back." My brother and I would turn around on our knees in the backseat to wave good-bye to our grandparents through the rear window of our car as my parents drove us away. I can still see them standing with my aunt Lucille, waving back from their front yard, moving their arms up and down at the shoulder, a gesture especially intended for children. Our windows were rolled down so we could hear my grandfather shouting, "Y'all come on back," as our car rounded the curve of the gravel driveway and we headed toward the pavement (the hard road, as we called it), sped up, climbed over the hill, and went out of sight.

My father was one of the first on the Thompson side of the family to leave the countryside for a town job. He and my mother were barely twenty years old when they married and moved in beside her mother in the county seat of Rocky Mount, Virginia, where I was born a year later. With both parents and my maternal grandmother working in town, I stayed regularly with my father's parents on their farm. When I was three—the year of the rooster encounter—we moved three hours away to Bristol, Virginia, in the southwest corner of the state on the Tennessee line, where, eventually my father would take a higher-paying job at the Northern Electric manufacturing plant. All I remember about it is that they made telephones, a fitting metaphor for the long-distance life my family began living, taking monthly trips back to Franklin County to visit family. The word *northern* also told a story: of factories moving down South from the Northeast to find workers fresh off the farm who were willing to work for cheaper wages. We were among both the beneficiaries and the targets of this new wave of industrialization.

Rural change is what my family talked about over their telephone lines, including jobs and distances apart and new opportunities and of children growing up in schools elsewhere. We also talked about everything on the farm and of the health of people and places back home. Then inevitably, at the end of the calls, my parents would promise the next trip back. We'll see you soon, they would say, and it was true. These regular visits were how I fell in love with farming. But mine was a love experienced through separation as much as proximity, with our living away from places and people I loved intensifying my affection for them.

Because we couldn't visit most of our relatives on our short trips back, my parents would run through a litany of family farms and houses along the roads as we passed them. I learned to repeat them as we approached. There's Roosevelt's farm, the Brammer place, Grandpa Smith's, Grandma Jamison's, Walter and Diane's, the Ikenberry farm, Aunt Clytie's and Uncle Chester's—the recitation of names undergirding my sense of place in the world through a car window, as though naming them could keep us connected, and driving by could preserve our farming past.

Heading from Bristol to Grandma's on Route 11 took us through all the small towns in the southwestern end of the Valley of Virginia: Abingdon, Marion, Wytheville, Dublin, Pulaski, Radford, and

Christiansburg, to name some of the most prominent. At Christiansburg, we turned east toward Floyd on Route 8, and after Floyd, we headed down the unmarked Shooting Creek Road. The roadway was named for the stream that had carved the narrow, dark hollow it ran through. Everyone in the family agreed that this curvy road was the quickest way to get back home by connecting in Endicott to Route 40, though Grandma joked the road builders had followed a snake's path when they made it.

Passing through Shooting Creek and the nearby hamlet called Endicott, by then mostly empty of people, meant revisiting fragments of the first chapter of our American farm story. My great-great-grandparents on two sides of our family had lived there deep in hollows in hand-hewn cabins, and had farmed with oxen and mules back when the road we were driving on was but a walking path. As we wound around the S-curves, my father pointed out the roads leading to where the first Thompsons, and our relatives, the Rakes, Smiths, Martins, Cannadays, and Shiveleys, had scratched out a living. It seemed almost unbelievable that people farmed those slopes. "The fields up there were so steep you'd have to put your corn seed into your rifle and shoot it up the hill to plant it," my grandma liked to repeat with a chortle.

Those Endicott ancestors were descendants of English and Scots-Irish immigrants who first came to the American colonies as indentured servants and later worked their way to landownership in the eighteenth century. Settlers of the Blue Ridge often came originally from plantations in Pennsylvania, Maryland, or northern Virginia. After paying off their debt, they headed southwest, following the Great Wilderness Road to the Virginia Blue Ridge, traveling as far as one could go by wagon road before staking their claims on some of the cheapest land, often part of huge, unexplored tracts granted to officers of the King. The first white settlers to move to what was then the edge of Virginia's western frontier in the mid-1700s encountered Indigenous peoples—the Saponi, Tuscarora, Cherokee, and others —whose ancestors had lived in those mountains for thousands of years before contact with Europeans. As whites overpowered these first inhabitants, they took over their hunting grounds and agricultural fields where they had grown corn, tobacco, and other crops. I am convinced this means I come from people who were once landless and then helped make others so. Displacement is a pattern repeated ad infinitum in human history, and few human lineages have lived completely free of its pain. The benefits of land tenure must always be tempered by the losses that made it possible.

American history is filled with such stories of families finding and settling land. Though my ancestors and their neighbors claimed some of the steepest and least accessible land in Virginia, they survived for generations in those hollows around Shooting Creek anyway. Working with neighbors, they made do in a mostly cashless economy supplemented only by periodic trips to market towns to sell chestnuts, corn whiskey, eggs, butter, and the occasional hog or steer they had raised on corn and mountain forage. Even as towns grew into cities in the East, they continued to grub a life from the steep, red, iron-rich soil, where they, and their offspring who survived childbirth and childhood diseases, lived by ingenuity, turning woods into farmsteads by hand, axe, and fire. In the end, the majority did not persist: By 1960, when I first remember traveling the road in the backseat of our car, only the shells of their homes and the ruins of their barns and fences remained. Some families had died out and were buried beside their homes. Others moved away to work in mines and mills. My great-grandparents had remained farmers, but they left the hollow to find better land. As we drove through the steep mountains where these farmers had once lived, our family's common refrain was how hard they had worked and how we were the beneficiaries of their toil.

Grandma and Grandpa Thompson's farm, some ten miles from Endicott and situated on more open, rolling land, represented the next chapter of our family's agricultural history. That chapter began when, as a young married couple, they accumulated enough money to buy equipment with which they could farm more acreage, first with horses and mules, then with tractors. They had entered a cash economy by the late 1920s, which made it possible for them to pay a bricklayer to construct their farmhouse and a neighbor to build their barn. Route

40, running from the deep mountains through Endicott, by their farm, and eventually to the county seat of Rocky Mount, was built and paved in the 1940s. The new proximity to markets afforded by the road helped my grandparents achieve relative success on their farm.

Though my grandparents made do for themselves by producing milk and beef and supplementing their farm income with side work, they never forgot the sacrifices their families made to get them where they were. They retained deep memories of Endicott, and I asked them to retell the details of their childhood every chance I got, even when their stories weren't easy to hear. My grandfather, for instance, often recalled his mother singing, but he also told us about waking up to see snow that had blown through the wooden shingles on the roof onto his bed on winter mornings, and about having just one pair of shoes, which he only wore for dressing up on Sundays or funerals. When he worked on his father's farm or walked to school he did so barefoot, except in the most extreme weather. It was "rough," he would say with a catch in his throat. In the winter months, when he hunkered close to the fire he tended in the basement woodstove, his hunched shoulders seemed to recount how cold he once felt growing up. He was extra careful to ensure that his grandchildren never got a chill. "Dress warm, now," he'd say before we went out to feed his farm animals, as if being cold was the worst thing he could imagine.

My grandpa had seen family members die in their beds waiting for a doctor to arrive from Rocky Mount, back when the road was barely passable even on a dry day. A Methodist mission several miles from his family's farm provided education for the children through the seventh grade and sometimes a nurse for the sick. But there was no hospital or high school, and no paved roads. Even if there had been a paved road, there were no vehicles that could reliably make the trip to the county seat. That Grandpa only made it to the seventh grade made him cherish what education meant for us. I sensed that his deep compassion for children was a direct result of the suffering he had witnessed. I loved him for his depth of feeling. I loved all of my grandparents in part because their attachment to places helped create my sense of home.

Before I was even five years old, I plunged into farm work with my grandfather, trying to copy his every movement. In turn, my effort yielded the kind of affirmations every child craves. "Look at Charles," Grandpa would say as I tried some Herculean task like lifting a sack of grain impossible for someone my age. "He's strong!" When the adults butchered hogs, I turned the handle of the manual sausage grinder until I had to be told it was time to stop. In the garden, I grasped the small hoe and tried to keep up with Grandpa as he chopped between the rows of sweet corn. Over time, I learned to run farm equipment by riding beside Grandpa on the tractor fender and lifting the handle that operated the three-point hitch when he gave the word; to drive a truck by first steering it in the hayfield, then riding beside Grandpa and shifting the gears when he instructed; to cut firewood by holding limbs in place for his next chainsaw cut; to build fences and sheds by holding the other end of his tape measure; to doctor animals by filling the syringe with penicillin and handing it to Grandpa so that he could give a sick cow a shot; to sharpen tools by turning the crank of the grinding wheel; and to repair machinery by finding the tools by name. "Go get me the three-eighths wrench," Grandpa would say, and I rummaged through the pile on the greasy workbench until it surfaced.

Grandma taught me how to turn home-raised meat and vegetables into meals. I used a biscuit cutter, mixed batter, and rolled pie dough before I could read. Soon I was pouring the leftover food scraps into the slop bucket at the basement steps, completing the whole cycle of growing vegetables from seed to basket to freezer to cast-iron frying pan and then back to the animals.

Through side-by-side work with the older generation, I learned details about farms my town friends had no inkling of. I remember arguing with two friends, neither of whom had rural relatives, that cows as well as bulls can have horns. We got the shop teacher to settle the score. I knew already because I had milked a Guernsey with horns, but my friends didn't believe me. I'm sure that few others in my junior high school in town had milked by hand, made butter with a hand churn, or learned how to tie the twine in a hay baler. As a result, I won most every argument about where food comes from. But it took me much longer to learn the harsh realities of farm economics, largely because as much as my family talked about farming, my relatives went silent on how little small farms paid. Because of this silence, I thought my father left the farm for a town job only because he wanted to. Believing that our living apart was merely a choice, I probably begged to stay later on Sundays a little too much. By the time I started to understand the larger economic picture that caused my parents to move away, my extended family's grip on their farms had already started to slip.

One of my first economic lessons came through my grandfather. He repeatedly asked me what I wanted to be when I grew up. Actually, he already had the answer figured out and reminded me every visit. I can hear him now: "You gonna be that vet?" to which I always replied, "Yes, sir," wanting to please him with all the determination I could muster. It's true, being a veterinarian was a job I could imagine for myself. I loved animals, and I agreed that the idea of driving around in a truck filled with medicines to visit farmers and work on their livestock was attractive. But I felt less than truthful telling Grandpa that was my first choice of vocation. So one Sunday, instead of answering yes, I decided to ask, "Why can't I be a farmer?" We both knew I wanted to be just like Grandpa, and so it seemed natural to me that he would want me to join him in his work.

Grandpa and I were sitting in aluminum lawn chairs with plastic webbing near the big cedar tree between the house and barn. The family had just finished playing some softball in the front yard, and afterward I was probably whittling on a cedar branch with Grandpa's pocketknife as I usually did on such occasions. He watched me for a few seconds, pondering how to answer his eldest grandson's query. Then he replied, "I know you like farming and working with animals and everything, but being a farmer doesn't pay much. A vet makes plenty of money. My vet has a big fine house in Rocky Mount. I think 'vetting' would be a good job because they can set their own hours and don't have to work so hard to make a living."

I always wanted to follow Grandpa everywhere he went, at times to my own endangerment. The only time my grandmother used a switch on me was when I was not yet five years old, for running toward Grandpa's two-ton truck as he was driving away. He had decided to leave me behind on an all-day trip to buy fertilizer that he would haul back and sell to individual farmers—one of his many sideline jobs. I just had to go, and I believed that if I could only jump onto the running board, he would have to stop and take me with him. So I dashed for the truck, and my grandmother, in a panic, ran after me, grabbing my collar just as I reached the end of the front walk. Then she reached up to the maple tree above, broke off a small branch with the leaves still attached, and switched my bare legs with it. I sulked for hours afterward. The switching barely hurt, but my feelings smarted for hours. I would have gone with Grandpa all night, I whimpered. I would have slept in the truck, anything to be with him.

Over time it became clear to me why he worked so hard at so many jobs. Hauling 10-10-10 fertilizer for long hours was just one of the ways Grandpa devised to support their farm. Along with fertilizer hauling, he also used his two-ton Chevrolet to transport neighbors' cattle to the stockyard, logs to sawmills, and sometimes even to haul gravel from the rock quarry to spread on neighbors' driveways. He did this all fitted around his usual farming demands. These sideline jobs were part his survival strategy; he could not have been a farmer without them. By the time I was twelve, he had also added the job of "carrying" the *Roanoke Times* in his farm pickup to some six hundred individual paper boxes every night, seven days a week. As I helped my aunt count up his monthly earnings that customers mailed him in envelopes, I began to absorb just how hard it is for a small farmer to make a living. Each of the little checks, which we counted and stamped FOR DEPOSIT ONLY, had to pay for the papers first, then the gas and truck upkeep. What was left would help pay the bills on the farm. I could do the math. Grandpa was sacrificing all of his time, even when farmers should be sleeping, to keep the farm going.

A child couldn't keep up. Grandpa's paper route started at eleven p.m. and ended past sunup around eight a.m., and on Sundays sometimes as late as nine a.m. He farmed by day, raising beef cattle, hay, hogs, chickens, and all the vegetables the family needed. He couldn't have slept more than three or four hours after supper and his bath, before getting up at ten at night and preparing to leave. Spending a few weeks over several summers on the overnight route and trying to help him farm by day taught me in the most direct way about the struggles of earning a living as a small farmer. After attempting, unsuccessfully, to keep my eyes open all night and falling asleep in the truck seat with rolled newspapers in my lap, I also slept through the next day's hay cutting and baling, only to awaken in the early afternoon in time for supper, feeling groggy and disappointed. Grandpa was often coming in from the field just as I was getting up. How unfair, I thought self-ishly, until I realized how hard he had been working while I was in bed. It all made me wonder, "Why isn't farming enough?"

I began to count it up. Not including the toll on Grandpa's body, every cost had to be subtracted from the total earnings on the farm. The dollar that each hay bale brought in had to be subtracted from the cost of Grandpa's New Holland baler, Ford tractor, the two-ton truck, the fertilizer, the labor, and gas, and so on. It didn't take sophisticated math skills to understand that the small farm income didn't cover the expenses. The newspaper earnings went toward balancing the farm budget. But that was no godsend, either.

I remember sitting on the arm of Grandpa's chair tracing my finger down the columns of numbers printed in the farm market futures in the *Roanoke Times* he held. I now know the numbers representing feeder calf prices were dictated by the Chicago Board of Trade and other national and international entities. They meant businesspeople living far from farms like the one owned by my grandparents were speculating on their future, and that of all farmers everywhere. The prices they set were based on the worldwide supply and demand of grain and meat, calculations that had nothing to do with individual productivity and did not weigh the outpouring of sweat against fossil fuel consumption. Nothing within the printed rows of dollar figures said anything about Grandpa's frugality, intelligence, or how many hours he worked around the clock. There were no people or places there, just numbers. Yet, as detached as the numbers appeared to be, those columns dictated whether farmers like those in my family might survive another year.

It was a world where cattle were counted by the hundredweight and dollar figures and corn came in trainloads, all distant calculations that affected the everyday prices mountain farmers got.

I asked Grandpa why people who work hard can't at least get back what it costs them to raise food. "Seems like most politicians don't care about the little man," Grandpa replied. His immediate family had benefited from Roosevelt's New Deal programs during the Great Depression, and for that reason he grew up believing that a government could act as a referee and keep economics fair . . . if the right people could be in charge. But they weren't, and still aren't. "Nowadays, the big companies get all the money in farming," he said. He never backed down on believing the government should help people, even later when Nixon and Reagan supporters in the family made fun of his politics. He was usually the only New Deal Democrat present during family discussions, and his gentleness made him an easy target. When anyone complained of high taxes, too much red tape, and government waste, he wouldn't raise his voice but would simply say that he appreciated schools and roads, the Social Security he'd been paying into, and the Medicare coverage that would become so essential later. He believed the "big wheel" needed to pay his fair share to help others. It was his way of talking about justice.

He had seen positive changes wrought by the Works Progress Administration and the Civilian Conservation Corps on the nearby Blue Ridge Parkway. He learned that sometimes people need a hand up, and when they do, the government can provide programs to help them. The same went for protecting the small producers and those who worked for hourly wage jobs. He espoused the same kind of ethics that favored the underdog when he saw us playing unfairly with one another. More than once he pulled me aside as the oldest and said gently under his breath, "Now, y'all don't be hard on the little fellers." His eyes would tear up slightly, and there was no way I could ignore his plea, because I knew he was thinking of his siblings who had died. His concern for the weaker ones and his gentle way of teaching fair play sank in deeper than any criticism of the government or lazy people I ever heard.

Author's grandfather Clifford Thompson.

Hauling | *1967*

"*H*ook that chain up high!" Grandpa said as he finally pushed the tailgate up to hold in the eight polled Hereford steers we would take to market early the next morning. I was eleven, and we had separated the eight from the rest of the herd, corralling the selected ones in the barn lot after calling them all in and feeding them. Before we could go in for supper ourselves, we coaxed and cajoled them into the truck, and the last act was getting the tailgate raised and chained shut. They stayed in the truck with plenty of hay to eat that night.

After eating breakfast the next morning before daylight, we drove in the truck to the Hollins Livestock Market on the other side of Roanoke, over an hour away. There, workers waiting at a dock helped us unload the steers and sent them down a chute on a concrete floor with high wooden rails. Running down the ramp, the young, stocky cattle disappeared into a maze of passages and stalls that were filled with a range of bovine sounds and strong smells of manure. When they had disappeared into the maze, we again raised the truck tailgate and secured its chain, drove the truck to the front parking lot, and went inside the front door to watch for our steers' arrival in the sales ring.

The day before their arrival at the stockyards, the steers had grazed on green pasture and drank water out of a stream on a small mountain farm. After the sale at Hollins, the steers could be headed to a feedlot in Nebraska by trailer, where they would stand on concrete with thousands of other cows, eating grain and drinking water from crusty troughs. I understood that was a chapter Grandpa had no control over. I knew he helped supply a demand for meat, and that without meat eaters those steers would never have been born in the first place. But that didn't excuse how the animals could be handled in the supply chain that followed his delivery and sale. And the meat ending up on American tables didn't absolve how my grandfather and the other small farmers who raised those animals were treated, either.

Passing through the front door and by the office, we entered another door to the sale area and sat in the bleachers overlooking the sawdust-floor ring where a few unidentified men scattered around the barn bid on hundreds of animals hauled in from farms in the surrounding counties. An hour or so later, Grandpa's eight auburn steers with white faces trotted through the gate and ran wild-eyed around the ring for about ten seconds. I recognized them right away, as the young men in the ring swung open a series of gates and jabbed at them gently with wooden canes to keep them trotting in a circle as the auctioneer sitting at a table with a microphone chanted his cadence, "Sixty-five, do I hear sixty-six?" The man beside the auctioneer pointed and shouted, "Yup!" One buyer in the barn had barely raised a finger. He got a nod from the auctioneer. "Sixty-seven, seven, seven? Lot number 105, sold for sixty-six." The bid was sealed just as the first steer found the open gate. All of them followed, thinking they'd escaped, and they disappeared down the chute and into a holding pen. From there they would be loaded into the trucks that were backed up to the loading dock.

Afterward, Grandpa and I went to have a hot dog and Coke in the café while the women in the sales office typed up his check. They checked the lot number against the buyer's and seller's numbers, calculated the total poundage into a dollar figure, and then subtracted the sales fee. After we ate, Grandpa picked up his envelope from the office window, thanked the women, and we headed back to the truck. In the truck cab, he slit open the envelope with his small penknife and silently read the price per pound and how many hundredweight he sold, his lips moving slightly as he read. He didn't talk about the total—he was too private for that—but I could see there was little pride in the transaction. I'm sure the sale at those low prices had barely covered his expenses, if that.

My grandfather had been demeaned, treated more like a low-wage employee than the producer and entrepreneur he was. I had started to understand why he thought being a veterinarian might be a better occupation for me, and also why my father had left the farm. This was plain wrong. Veterinarians and tractor salespeople set their prices at a level that pays them for their time and expenses. In contrast, farmers like Grandpa take most of the risks of production of food and invest their entire livelihood in getting products to market, while their returns come back to them like a gambler's unlikely winnings in a casino. With every trip to the market, they wager on whether their returns will be enough to pay the bills. The hands are dealt to them by someone else holding the deck. And the house always wins in the end.

★ ★ ★

I was in my final year of college when my father and mother decided to leave their jobs to return to the farm to help my grandparents. As it turned out, my dad liked farming more than he had let on. My parents dipped into their savings to make his move back to farming possible. I cheered the venture because it meant the family could possibly preserve the farm for another generation and perhaps someday even give me a chance at farming, too. Unfortunately, their joint endeavor lasted less than a year when my dad realized that after buying their first batch of feeder calves from a dairy farm, they could never earn back the initial investment and feed costs, let alone contribute to supporting two households. Instead of continuing to throw good money after bad, as he said, my father started a used-car lot two miles from the farm. By selling cars, he could set the prices to cover expenses, which he did. Almost immediately, T&S Auto Sales began to yield more reliable profits by selling secondhand vehicles on an acre lot beside the highway than 150 acres could by raising food.

Though no one voiced it at the time, that unsuccessful venture with the feeder calves spelled the end of the Thompson family's tenure in farming. Our agricultural genealogy, likely stretching backward in time to when Europeans first husbanded animals—and that included immigrants settling the Appalachians searching for land—would now, with my grandparents' deaths, come to an end. In my grandfather's lifetime, the collective dreams of generations past had been achieved and dashed.

After both my grandparents died, my father and uncle and two aunts met with a realtor and announced they had signed an agreement on a price for the farm. No one talked about the land being a family farm or about preserving it for posterity. They only spoke of the division of the proceeds into fourths, with everything remaining as equitable as possible. They would sell the homestead through a realtor. "There was no way to make a living at farming," they repeated often to help them get over their sadness at the loss. No one could argue with them, for every one of us knew firsthand how hard my grandparents had worked and how little, but the house and land itself, the family had to show for their labors. The land continued to increase in value, not because of the farming income it could bring in, but for the other uses for which it could be sold. "They aren't making any more land," Grandma had liked to say.

Not long after the farm went up for sale, a doctor bought the whole place in one piece and opened a firing range on it. He and his family made the farmhouse into their office and used the fields where Grandpa had planted a garden and fruit trees for their bull's-eye targets and skeet throwers. Fortunately for us, the land continued to look like a farm, and they even ran some cattle on the pasture; but their income, avoiding the gamble of farming altogether, came from customers shooting at targets. Relatives who have since stopped by the farm say the new owners are quite welcoming and have given them tours of the entire place, including inside the house.

I have not turned into the driveway since the place sold, however. I prefer to remember the farm as it was when I last saw my grandfather passing by the old rusted farm bell on his way toward the barn to start his old blue Ford tractor, his frame slightly bent in his later years, but his gait spry. I want to remember the sound of his voice as he stood at the fence to call his cattle in the high-pitched falsetto voice that came from some other place in our distant past. It seemed to be from another tongue, some other land. "Soo-cow, sook, sook, come on!" he shouted until all the cattle came running toward him, as trained as a passel of hunting dogs, all of them knowing there would be a payoff of something to eat. The cows answered in kind, as though echoing his call. "Soo, sook!" they replied in their own high-pitched voices as they trotted up the path toward the barn. It was magical.

★ ★ ★

A few years after the sale of the place Grandpa had named Twin Maples Farm, my mother's first cousin, a lifelong farmer, lost his grandmother's (my great-grandmother Jamison) farm to foreclosure. The place where she had saved me from the rooster was sold at auction to a developer who moved quickly to build houses all over the land. The builder gave the development a pastoral name—something akin to Mountain View Acres—to capitalize on the farm image that so many want to hold on to as they move onto an acre or two. Of course, the new construction that followed meant that any future agricultural potential for the place was dead. Other farms in the area met similar fates. A few neighboring farmers bought up land in order to increase their production, but even as those acres remained in agriculture, the people who once lived nearby were disappearing. Though displacement has always been present in agriculture since the beginning of European farming, small farming communities in America once provided at least a counterbalance to the losses of agriculture. Our lives were a part of the farming narrative that included family and community. Now with families selling or dying out, the rural ethos shifted toward profit and acquisition, and the industrial model of agriculture we came to call agribusiness became the norm.

In retrospect, it is clear that my family's departure from their land was part of a nationwide hemorrhaging of farmers that intensified after World War II and nearly bled out by the 1980s and early 1990s. Back in 1940, a year before the war started, over thirty million people, nearly a third of the US population, still lived on farms. By 1960, around the time when I went out to explore Grandma Jamison's poultry lot and we moved to Bristol, the number of farmers had been halved, to just over fifteen million Americans or 8 percent of the population. Ten years later, in 1970, when I was thirteen and riding with Grandpa on his paper route, the working farm population had shrunk to 9.7 million, or 4.6 percent of the labor force. By 1980, the year after my college graduation, when my father had decided to sell used cars for a living two miles down the road from my grandparents' place, the percentage had declined to only 3.4 percent of the American population. Today, the number of farm owners has shrunk to only 1 percent. The US prison population far outnumbers its farmers.

Though people have always left farms and moved elsewhere in search of a better life, there had never been an exodus as immense and as final as the one that came to be called the American Farm Crisis of the 1980s. On the positive side of the economic ledger, the three decades prior witnessed unprecedented growth of manufacturing, new jobs, and increased American prosperity in the burgeoning postwar economy. On the other side lay rural America's pain and loss. As farmers departed from their traditional occupation, hundreds of thousands of families nationwide were forced to relinquish ties to land that they had scrambled to hold for generations. When they left in the 1980s, families' farm tenure was ending for good. Whole communities began drying up. Too many farm families, including those of the Blue Ridge, suffered in silence, never talking to other family members or neighbors about how it felt to lose their attachments to land and its history. This silence was to be replaced by a deeper despair once they were gone.

One major break in the silence in Virginia came at a formative time for me, however. In 1978, when I was twenty-one years old, I was driving toward Richmond when I witnessed the Tractorcade. It wasn't the first time in American farm history that farmers had protested unfair policies, but it was the first time I saw firsthand any expression of collective discontent or uprising.

As I topped a hill on the four-lane highway, a line of tractors that looked a mile long came into view. The machines were headed in the same direction I was, northward on the right-hand side of the road. All makes, sizes, and colors of tractors were in formation, a convoy of farmers on a mission. As I approached slowly in the left lane, I could see that the tractors were emblazoned with protest signs identifying the group as the AMERICAN AGRICULTURE MOVEMENT. As I passed them, I read other posters taped to the tractor cabs announcing they were headed toward Washington, DC in protest. One read, "Every time a farmer sells a commodity, he or she goes a little deeper in debt." I waved, trying to convey my solidarity. I knew from my own family how hard farmers worked for no money, and by that time in my life I knew more who were suffering from the effects of that grim reality. I wanted the farmers in the Tractorcade to know I had a stake in their cause.

Grandpa's little Ford tractor with no cab would have been dwarfed by that parade of big equipment owned by farmers hailing from the Piedmont and Coastal Plains of Virginia and the Carolinas, but I knew his farm was just as affected as any. What was new for me was the farmers' open challenge to the agricultural status quo, and their demand that the federal government do something to address their economic plight. The signage announced that government policies favored corporations, and that family farmers, most all of them "little people" in the national scheme of things, knew they were suffering because of unfair competition from an agribusiness that was propped up with subsidies. The middlemen and the corporations were siphoning off all the profits, which threatened all independent farmers, even the big family farms. Though my brief encounter with the American Agriculture Movement (AAM) Tractorcade was only a quick, drive-by lesson in farm activism, it planted ideas in me that would germinate and grow in the years to come. I honked my horn at one of the drivers and waved one more time as I whizzed on beyond them, all the while trying to decipher why that scene made such an impression on me.

Today I understand. I was born at the right time and in the right place for farming to become a central part of my identity. I was closer to agriculture than the vast majority of my friends, and was definitely closer than the average town dweller, even in Virginia's small hamlets. Yet the timing of my birth also meant my coming of age coincided with the demise of every farm in our family: Every named place; every piece of land that served as a repository of our stories told to me by relatives; and every farm I had ever played or worked on as a child, was dying. Though I had never been a farm owner I, too, had experienced a farm crisis. I was grieving.

Since childhood, I had cherished and collected the details of my farm relatives' lives, and of their land. When both went away, they did so too quickly, too quietly, leaving no map of where to go from there and no instructions on what to do with my memories. I had no obvious place to apply the knowledge I had gained from their legacy, and knew no tangible way that I could pass on what I had learned. Then as if from somewhere far off, I heard my grandmother Jamison's voice again shouting, "You get back there!" I listened to the faint memory of her voice, knowing this time it was meant for me.

Interstate 26, mountain farm, and doublewide trailer in Madison County,
North Carolina. Photograph by Rob Amberg.

Culling | *1968–69*

*I*n 1960, when my father began working as a foreman in the Monroe Calculator manufacturing plant in Bristol, we moved into a small house in a circular subdivision built for people like my parents—young, increasingly mobile, postwar, middle class, and white—many of them with late baby boomer children like me. My parents chose that particular small city in part because my father's sister and her husband had already found work there. After my parents bought a house just a few doors away from them, my brother and I saw our cousins almost every day, and we all grew up as close as siblings.

Eight years later, in 1969, as I turned thirteen—when my cousin Bruce and I were nearly joined at the hip—my father got a better job at Brunswick Corporation fifty miles to the northeast in Marion, Virginia. Brunswick had been attracted to the Virginia mountains partly because of the oak and maple timber growing in the surrounding forests, which made perfect lumber for their pool tables and bowling alleys. The corporation had grown fast because it supplied recreational goods across the nation just as newfound leisure time in American suburbs allowed for the surge in demand for these products. In addition, Brunswick had secured a government contract to make metal field hospitals that could be dropped by parachute from cargo planes into Vietnam during the war.

The year 1969 was a good one, at least for white families geographically separated from the widespread tension of cities, and with no one serving in Vietnam. That year, the average income in the United States went up 9 percent over the year before, and the overall unemployment rate dropped to 3.5 percent.* In today's currency, the minimum wage per hour was over ten dollars. The federal tax rate had gone as high as 91 percent for those making over $400,000 per year in 1960, and was still at 71 percent for anyone making over $200,000 in 1970.† Those taxes both reduced the gap between the rich and poor and paid for infrastructure improvements like new interstate highways. Factories were hiring, and the resulting economic boom reached even to Appalachia, at least to places where there were good roads like the one that passed through Marion. Though the language of industrial recruiting for southwestern Virginia didn't say so openly, likely the most attractive aspect of the place for the factory owners who relocated there was the plethora of hardworking farm exiles from our region who needed work and were thankful to get it. Our region's relative quietude and dearth of unions had to be factors as well.

As a result of the hiring boom, 1969 was the year our family became securely ensconced in the American middle class. That year my dad bought a new yellow Impala with a black vinyl top, upgrading from a Corvair, which gave our morale a boost even as the national mood turned violent and fearful. Though Lyndon Johnson's programs had previously addressed both coalfield poverty and urban blight, Richard Nixon beat Johnson's chosen successor, Hubert Humphrey, by the thinnest of margins in 1968. Many credit Nixon's win to his invocation of "law and order" couched within his racist Southern Strategy.

President Johnson, using the tax money garnered mostly from the wealthy, had also initiated his signature economic program, the War on Poverty in 1964–65, an initiative designed to address the

---

* Kimberly Amaded, "Unemployment Rate by Year Since 1929 Compared to Inflation and GDP," *The Balance*, February 28, 2019, https://www.the balance.com/unemployment-rate-by-year-3305506.

† "United States Federal Income Tax Brackets and Maximum Tax Rates: 1950–1980," Stanford University Course Hub, https://web.stanford.edu /class/polisci120a/immigration/Federal Tax Brackets.pdf.

plight of the poor, including whites in the mountain South. His administration had also started Medicaid, VISTA (Volunteers in Service to America), the Job Corps, and Community Action Programs designed to help with education, community development, and health care.* During those years it was common for national news reporters to enter the coal camps a county away from us to report on poverty and the effects of Johnson's new aid. At roughly the same time, a Job Corps training site for young women opened up in an old college in downtown Marion. As our town was one of the brighter spots on the mountain region's economic map, it made sense to bring the unemployed to Marion for training.

The year 1968 had brought the beginning of Nixon's corruption, the assassinations of Dr. Martin Luther King, Jr. and Robert F. Kennedy, and the Tet Offensive, the Vietnam War's bloodiest campaign. As my family was settling into the relative security of my father's new job, demonstrators were hitting the streets all across America to protest our racial apartheid, an unjust war, and for those influenced by such leaders as Dr. King and Malcolm X, the confluence of both. Students on campuses nationwide—including Virginia Tech a hundred miles to our north in Blacksburg, Virginia —were in an uproar.[†]

We watched coverage of civil rights and antiwar protests on the news brought to our living room by Walter Cronkite, Chet Huntley, and David Brinkley. One detail I noticed on the news was that some African American leaders like Stokely Carmichael and Bob Moses marched wearing bib overalls, which was also the uniform of rural men I had known. Years later, I would come

---

* Dylan Matthews, "Everything You Need to Know about the War on Poverty," *Washington Post*, January 8, 2014, www.washingtonpost.com/news /wonk/wp/2014/01/08/everything-you-need-to-know-about-the-war-on -poverty/?utm_term=.83f1faeca71c.

† "The Hahn Years (1962–74)," *Historical Digest*, 2017, www.unirel.vt.edu /history/historical_digest/hahn_years.html.

to understand how the marchers had used those rural clothes to hark back to the history of African American enslavement and sharecropping often connected with the expression "forty acres and a mule," a phrase that would later speak to me so forcefully. Even as an adolescent, I understood some of the symbolism, and I also began to comprehend some of the commonalities shared by my rural white relatives and rural Black people long before I had the words to articulate them.

Right after the news, as if to calm any fears it raised, came *Leave It to Beaver, The Andy Griffith Show,* and other TV shows depicting rural and suburban white families living in American security. Distant from racial unrest and antiwar uprisings, we nestled into our warm brick home to watch the programs and, in FDR's words, to be "free from fear," secure in the belief that the factory jobs that had replaced agricultural work were going nowhere anytime soon.

Though only a generation later we would learn that the economy's pivot away from traditional rural life and toward manufacturing was not the permanent fix we had believed it was, the initial growth of factories was a godsend for my father. He had earned an associate's degree at Ferrum College, a school that began as a Methodist Church mountain mission where my grandmother had earned her high school diploma. He became one of the lucky ones whose move away from farming led to his climb up the company ladder, eventually to a supervisory role. After commuting the fifty miles from Bristol, he chose, with minimal family input, to buy a little brick ranch house on Route 11 in a hamlet named Atkins. We moved there just as I started seventh grade. The house was seven miles from the county seat of Marion, fifty feet or so from the highway, and within a few hundred yards of the new interstate. With a carport and a short, paved driveway that connected directly to the larger yellow-lined Route 11, the house was perfectly oriented for commuting, and our life there became focused on driving—to work, to school, to sports practices and games, to shop for groceries, and to visit relatives elsewhere. The plain brick house felt lonely from the first time I saw it.

Our transience was one big reason why going to my grandparents' place felt so good when we finally arrived there each month. I never felt lonely or lost while my family worked and ate together, played cards and board games at night, or at bedtime, when the children slept together on quilt pallets on the floor. Surrounding us was 150 acres of hilly land all owned by my grandparents, with no neighboring houses in sight. Close up, that scene might have resembled a Rockwell painting, though if you pulled back to examine that household's position in the larger economy, the scene was anything but secure.

By the late 1960s, agriculture had experienced more than a decade of rapid mechanization of nearly every farm task. With bigger machines came an exponential increase in the use of the agrochemicals that Rachel Carson had alerted the world to in her 1962 book, *Silent Spring*. Growth in production also led to lower market prices, which put pressure on every small farmer to increase acreage or go out of business. Though the slightly lower grocery prices that resulted from the new boosts in production were a small relief for families dependent on paychecks, for those who struggled to make a living on small acreages, and who had little chance of expanding, the era brought a precipitous decline in farm income.

In the 1960s and '70s, decision makers in government and agribusiness forcefully hastened rural communities toward farm consolidation. Gone were the programs of the 1930s and '40s when the USDA gave loans to sharecroppers to help them stay in farming, and for the masses to buy small parcels as the Founding Fathers had envisioned. Instead, the government, influenced by large corporations, began fostering the rise of factory farms. As early as 1971, Nixon's secretary of agriculture, Earl Butz, proclaimed that farmers must either "get big or get out," sending a harsh rejection notice to the yeomen whose survival had once been a government mandate.

Our family didn't have to stretch to see the changes coming to farms we knew, but still we avoided talking about them. We preferred the close-up view of the food on our plates, and extolling the quality of the tasty meats and vegetables that Grandpa raised and Grandma cooked. Those biscuits, how light and fluffy! Country ham, homegrown! Corn on the cob! Lima beans! Our own tomatoes! Despite being one of those families already displaced by change, for about forty-eight hours each month we continued to act like farm people—eating the produce, working to help build a fence or get up hay, and telling stories about life on the land. Above all, we children felt securely at home.

No one in our family articulated why my father and his siblings had no choice but to look elsewhere for jobs. But one could have traced those major changes that had come to our lives by following the car tracks heading out of my grandparents' gravel driveway by Sunday afternoon or Monday morning.* By then all four of their grown children, even the two youngest still living at home as adults, would be heading to work at off-farm jobs. Their choice had been to either move away or face long commutes every day. The miles on their odometers showed how farm succession had ended for us. Though two still lived at home, there was no future for them there. And even as we settled into our quilts on Friday or Saturday night, our farmer grandfather was headed out in his pickup to acquire the load of Sunday papers he would deliver all night long. While we were eating banana pudding or some other dessert after supper, Grandpa was climbing the stairs to take a bath and sleep a few hours before leaving. As we lay down on the floor, we could hear the gravel in the driveway crackling under his truck tires. We internalized how hard farmers had to work, even as we giggled ourselves to sleep. Deep down we knew this scene was fleeting. Children are never as naive as they pretend.

From such scenes, it is easy to guess why American manufacturing reached a pinnacle of productivity in the postwar period between

---

* Sociologist Charles J. Galpin studied just this kind of road turning in 1915, before there were paved roads to most farms. See: *The Countryside in the Age of Capitalist Transformation.*

the late 1940s and 1973.* Farm people who learned to work hard at home helped create America's postwar heyday as they transferred their agricultural work ethic to work in factories. We became part of the ongoing transferal of values when, on Sunday afternoon, two carloads of us would head back to the Interstate 81 corridor in the southern end of the Valley of Virginia where we would wave to our cousins, turn off toward Atkins, and take our farm lives and park them in the little house.

At Atkins, the Virginia Valley is sandwiched between the Blue Ridge to the east and the Alleghenies to the west where, by the time we moved there, the interstate corridor had been built up with factories and warehouses. In the mid-nineteenth century, the Norfolk and Western (Virginia) railroad laid its tracks through the valley, following the middle fork of the Holston River. Then came Route 11, following the same river bottom. The 1960s brought the interstate alongside, but instead of meandering along the river as the previous highway had, the new superhighway cut through mountains, raised low spots, and paved a way for our region to connect to the rest of nation. The roads brought the factories, followed by the factory workers and their dwellings. Atkins, once a sleepy rural farming hamlet, became one of our county's main industrial areas.

As the land along the roads filled up with new buildings, the only farmland left in Atkins was back up on the hills away from the road, often landlocked and growing up in weeds. Behind our single row of five houses was a blocked-in old pasture that had grown up in broomsedge, blackberry canes, and scrub pines. One last old farmhouse on our side of the road sat back from the newer houses by several hundred feet. Despite its proximity to our house, its orientation had been toward the fields around it, where people stayed home and worked the land. Now it sat beyond a chasm of

---

* Robert J. Gordon, "Revisiting U.S. Productivity Growth over the Past Century with a View of the Future," The National Bureau of Economic Research, March 2010, www.nber.org/papers/w15834.

time and economics, irrelevant to our car-focused lives as it fell into disrepair.

An older unmarried Pentecostal preacher named Ms. Robinette still lived in the old farmhouse when we moved to the house beside her. Her parents had been farmers and she inherited the place when they died. By the time we moved in, her farm's outbuildings and barns were already falling down. The cattle that had once grazed up on the hill were long gone. The farmers had died and agriculture was not coming back. When I mowed Ms. Robinette's yard in the summer for a few dollars a week, mine was the only quasi-agricultural act still associated with the place. Because she knew me, she didn't mind my squeezing through the rusted and broken barbed-wire fence behind her house to walk up to the old fields to explore with my dog.

Climbing the hill, I would turn to look back at the narrow pass where the railroad track and the highways all squeezed against one another in the narrow river valley. From there, I could watch the whining southbound trucks rounding a curve from behind the mountain as they hauled goods toward Bristol; from behind hills to my left came the northbound semis, where they crossed the bridge over the river and the railroad and headed toward Roanoke. Standing in that overgrown field, I witnessed one of our region's main arteries pumping goods from our factories and warehouses into one big American economic circulatory system.

For a dislocated youth in search of meaning in a landscape in transition, watching the hurried movement of goods up and down the highways only added to my angst. As I walked out alone trying to imagine my way in the world, repeating the age-old rite of separation from parents, I felt that there was no place to ground me. With the empty pasture behind and the vehicles in motion in front, the little brick houses all lined in a row on the highway were like dinghies floating on a rough sea. They gave my eyes and spirit nothing to hold on to. The transportation corridor before me brought the whole of the nation within reach, but it only communicated distance and anonymity, not location, purpose, and identity. The drivers whizzing by had no faces, no names. My grandparents, in contrast, liked to name every car that passed by their farm on Route 40, guessing where the occupants they could name had been and where they were going.

The interstate semis were painted with ads to entice people to identify with a brand or store. Often, they displayed a picture of a farm or farm animal to advertise their food products. One I remember well was the smiling, grocer's-hat-wearing cartoon pig on the side of the Piggly Wiggly trucks. Though perhaps a dozen family households in our family back in Franklin County were still attempting to make a living by farming at the time, the food system those trucks were part of was already so industrialized that I had no idea how any food got to our Piggly Wiggly in Marion. Brand loyalties were built by logos and TV jingles, not by relationships with people or the food they produced. The stores had nothing to do with the fields and cows I knew by name. Hearing the whine of the trucks going by reminded me the ground beneath my feet in Ms. Robinette's weedy old pasture had also lost its song. While I could sing the food slogans as well as anyone, they gave me no sense of belonging anywhere.

In 1969, I turned thirteen in that brick house; I was in the heat of adolescence. Vietnam raged on, Neil Armstrong and his crew walked on the moon, the first jumbo jet, the Boeing 747, made its transatlantic flight, and the Beatles played their last concert on the roof of Apple Records. It was also the year the three-day extravaganza called Woodstock exploded onto the national news. Even in my small Virginia mountain enclave, the idea of youths gathering outdoors to celebrate music, protest the Vietnam War, and find their place on Max Yasgur's dairy farm, made an impact on me.

My antennae were up, both on my new five-band transistor radio I had gotten for Christmas and on my youth receptors tuned to cultural paradigm shifts, and I started receiving their signals. The message of the powerful songs I was listening to from Chicago decried war and the industrial complex that funded it. The powerful message I received was that we had sold our souls for all the wrong values. Even in Atkins, where too many of the students riding my bus lived in unpainted houses, and the families of at least one of my classmates still used an outhouse, the fact that young people were turning their backs on corporate America and had embraced a return to Mother Earth resonated with me. I was too young and disconnected to join the counterculture directly, but I did tune in to its songs and daydream right along with the movement.

By the time I started high school, we had moved into Marion proper. I began growing out my hair and wearing the uniform of would-be yeoman farmers: patched jeans, work shirts, and boots, like Bob Dylan, Neil Young, and others who wore them on the album covers I saw after I persuaded my mother to let me join the Columbia House Record Club—one cent for twelve LPs. I embraced the antiestablishment message of the rock artists, though it wasn't lost on me that the style I was seeing was also reminiscent of the clothes my grandfather and other rural men wore when they worked outside. I had tried to dress like Grandpa all my life. Now I was finding hippie clothing by rummaging through his old work clothes that were hanging on nails down in his basement. I also found and started wearing my uncle's military field jacket from when he was stationed in Germany. My look was rebellious and a throwback to my family's past at the same time.

By the tenth grade I had "joined in a rock and roll band," as Joni Mitchell sang in her anthem "Woodstock"; and right on cue with her song, I had also begun dreaming of getting "back to the land to set my soul free." The difference for me was that the land I imagined going back to, and then started depicting in my art projects in school, looked a lot like mountain farms I knew: rolling fields bounded by mountains, often dotted with picturesque fencerows, old gray barns, and cattle grazing. Getting "back to the garden," in other words, had a specific locus for me. A return to nature that may have seemed a radical departure for many urban and suburban youths was for me reminiscent of entering the old blurry pictures that my grandmother had shown me of farm life back in Endicott and Shooting Creek. The old patched bib overalls my ancestors wore out of necessity in those pictures had become a symbol of rejection of the buttoned-up establishment.

My grandmother, a proud woman who ironed every article of clothing her children wore, and always bought the best quality she could afford, never quite understood my clothing downgrade. Hadn't she worked so hard to live beyond her parents' and her own struggle out of poverty? Now, just two generations later, I was already going in reverse. It made no sense to her. She politely mentioned my hair and my whiskers, letting me know she noticed, and she bought me some nice clothes to try to entice me to go in the other direction, but she never let me see any disapproval.

I knew I was always welcome in her kitchen. And there, sharing with Grandpa a cup of coffee and a country ham biscuit she had made by hand in the old wooden dough bowl and cooked in her white enameled stove with the black clock face and dials, I was more in touch with who I was than anywhere else on earth. My grandparents' home place provided the steadiest foundation on which I could stand, even as I questioned, or sometimes lamented, America's changing landscape.

Carolina farm auction. Photograph by Rob Amberg.

Propagating | *1972*

*H*oping to find what getting back to the garden might mean for me, I made a key discovery in the beginning of my sophomore year of high school. During the first week, otherwise a blur, the high school's greenhouse suddenly seemed to appear from behind a row of white pines in back of the gym, an image from a world I had overlooked my entire freshman year. The greenhouse was part of the "Vo-Ag" curriculum designed for the vocational and agricultural trades. When I found out I was eligible to take courses out there, I signed up for Horticulture One right away.

By doing so, I was about to cross the divide between the college-bound world and its parallel universe designed for blue-collar youths. Or maybe I should call them the blue-jacket youths, as they wore corduroy Future Farmers of America jackets with the trademark yellow emblem on the back—an eagle perched on a cross section of an ear of corn. By 1973, the Future Farmers of America organization already seemed passé, even in our small-town high school, though some of the members defiantly held on. Instead of surrendering, the national FFA leaders had tried to make their organization trendier by calling members "agri-businessmen" instead of farmers. The business emphasis paralleled the trend our guidance counselor had told us about: namely, that anyone who wanted to be successful had to go to college, including farmers. The strong message school administrators preached to youths of my generation was that anyone who remained traditional was destined to be left behind. In that light, the Vo-Ag program justified its existence by arguing it was preparing students for industrialized farming, as sophisticated as any factory in the city. Everyone has to eat no matter what, and the FFA students would be prepared to make the necessary changes as farms began to operate with the efficiency of assembly lines. Even if robots did the farming, we would need technicians to operate the switches and to keep the machines running. And those technicians needed agribusiness training, because, the implication was, farmers as we knew them would soon be gone.

Meanwhile, the counterculture I'd started gravitating toward conveyed an opposite message about farms: namely, that the old farmers who wore overalls, grew their own food, and maybe even worked with draft horses, were cool. Woodstock youths wrapped in blankets, lying in farm mud, or skinny-dipping in the pond by the barn; R. Crumb's Mr. Natural sitting on a tractor; James Taylor on the cover of his 1970 album *Sweet Baby James* leaning on a fence post in a work shirt: Those were images that spoke to me, even as the counselors pushed me in the opposite direction. I became captivated by urban youths who were starting to throw off what they said were the pretentious trappings of a society bent on destroying itself. That was the camp I was headed for when the school greenhouse suddenly appeared to me.

The horticultural classroom was anything but countercultural, and the people I met inside were not exactly my tribe. In fact, the conventional wisdom among my college-bound peers was that most of the Vo-Ag kids were losers, the ones administrators might call "at-risk youths" who were just one minimum-wage job away from dropping out of school. To many of my town friends, they were just rednecks and greasers; and though all of them were white, which afforded them a modicum of privilege in America, the college-bound still considered them inferior. But I had known some of them from back in the seventh grade in Atkins. I had gone to Julian's house a couple of afternoons after school and met his family. I knew his father was sick, and had seen how, even though their house was old and they used an outhouse, the family seemed almost grateful that I had befriended their son, which made me feel embarrassed. I also remembered that my Atkins classmate Jean—one of the prettiest girls I'd ever seen at the time—lived in an old, grayed weatherboard dwelling with broken siding, and how when our school bus stopped directly in front of her house, she lingered at her mailbox so those of us looking out of the bus windows would not see which one she entered. I found it easy to figure out which one it was. But I also knew her mother bought Jean very nice clothes and came to the school functions to support her daughter when she was not working. I didn't have to understand the root causes of poverty well to know that blaming individuals for how they looked or what they wore or how their house looked was wrong.

I got why the Vo-Ag boys wore real work clothes that were cheaper and more polyester than the all-cotton pretend work clothes of the college-bound students. I knew why their boots had steel toes. I understood why their hair, even if they started growing it long over their collars, sent a different message from mine, more like Elvis's long hair and sideburns than the Beatles' look. What all of it conveyed to me was that the FFA boys were from different histories and places from that of the college-bound—and they were trying to hold on to their rural world with all they had, even as their lives were becoming unmoored.

For many of the "shop guys," even those from areas as far away as twenty or thirty miles from Marion, rural life could not support their dreams. Although some still lived on farms, most were now starting to get the message that they couldn't make a living at it in the future. Even if they lived on family land, most would put up a trailer on the property and work elsewhere. If they had fathers who worked as mechanics, plumbers, or bulldozer operators, they were lucky because they could learn a trade from a relative and still live at home. For many who would end up working with their hands, school seemed to have little to do with their future.

For that reason, Vo-Ag became a holding ground for boys on their way to the work world they seemed all too eager to join. Work for most would mean heading to factories so that they could earn enough money to get married and live in a place near family. Many liked the idea of buying big stereos, cars and pickups with loud mufflers to work on in the yard, no one telling them what to do, burgers and deer meat to grill, and beer to drink on the weekends. With the unemployment rate low, and the buying power of the minimum wage still strong, some of the boys believed they could survive even if they quit school, at least as long as the factories were hiring. As far as anyone knew, those manufacturing plants were stable. Teachers struggled to keep them in school, begging them to wait for just a few more years until graduation. Diplomas might give them a chance at something else besides working on a factory line. Vocational classes—hands-on and easy to pass—would count.

The Vo-Ag boys had their morning homeroom period out in the shop rather than in the main school. They took General Ed in their own classrooms, while the college-prep students took courses like calculus and advanced chemistry in the heart of the school. While my cohort attended afternoon classes, the vocational boys were often headed out to work for half a day earning money, one foot already out of the door.

Though I now lived in town, I knew from living in Atkins and from relatives in Franklin County that rural life was under siege. My experience taught me that when the shop boys acted tough, the loss of rural life was likely one strong reason why. The boys' ornery and aggressive attitudes, in other words, went deeper than testosterone. If they took to fighting, which was common, it was in part because they knew the meek were not to be the inheritors of the earth any-time soon. They knew that our region was in trouble. Even the ones who still farmed knew their families were being pushed off the land. Some pushed and shoved back. The college-bound and the "uppity" were often their target.

Of course, none of us so-called uppity college-bound students, or our parents, had anything to do with the storms blowing through our rural communities. Every one of the inhabitants of small-town Marion or Atkins or Franklin County, or anywhere in rural America, was being propelled toward the future by the same harsh winds that we could not control. Those winds, some of which came from Wall Street or the Chicago trading boards, or even distant forces like international grain trading with Russia or their invasion of

Czechoslovakia, blew from parts far away and seemingly unrelated to our day-to-day lives or choices. The difference between us was that some of the lucky ones could catch those winds of change in their sails and get blown away toward other horizons, while many of the Vo-Ag boys—acting tough and resisting change—hunkered down to wait it out. They would do their best to hold their ground even as the coming economic gales blew their whole world away.

Charlie Thompson inside Marion Senior High School's greenhouse.

Germinating | *1973*

*A*s I walked into the misty, rain forest–like environment of the greenhouse, surrounded by jade plants, spider plants, and cacti, I felt more at ease than at any point in my entire school experience to that point. It was as if I was walking into a class for a language I already knew but had never risked speaking around my town peers. A part of me that had remained dormant began to perk up inside. And that I would get academic credit for working with plants that I loved was a major bonus. On the first day after orientation when we were taking cuttings and transplanting them, I knew I was in the right place.

My horticulture teacher, Mr. Waddle, was a gentle and affable man with slicked-back hair, simple polyester clothes, lace-up Hush Puppies, and a narrow clip-on tie. He must have thought a "long-hair" like me an oddity in his class, but he took me in anyway. Before long, I learned alongside my classmates how to propagate and grow all the popular ornamentals, including succulents like aloe and jade plants. We grew homecoming mums for the dance, and poinsettias for the school to sell at Christmas. We planted vegetable bedding plants that would be for sale to the general public in the spring. But this side of horticulture wasn't my reason for being in the class. I just wanted to be near anything that had to do with farming.

One day, having arrived early to class, I noticed a knee-high stack of *Organic Gardening* magazines on the floor beside Mr. Waddle's cluttered desk. I had never heard of the publication before, but I was drawn to the colorful photograph of the vegetable garden on the cover of the top copy. I picked it up and started browsing through it back at my desk. A few minutes later, Mr. Waddle walked in, looked around the classroom, and noticed what I was reading. I looked up sheepishly, afraid that I had overstepped my bounds. But he smiled and asked if I'd like to take a few issues home with me. I took him up on the offer and started reading the magazines cover-to-cover that night. It was unusual for me to elect to read anything except liner notes inside of album covers, but this experience was different.

I had probably heard the word *organic* before, but now suddenly I had found an entire cadre of people enthused about making compost, avoiding pesticides and commercial fertilizers, and growing amazing food—at least it looked amazing in the photographs. In their own attractive and pleasant way, Rodale Press's growers were pushing back against the entire agribusiness complex. I had never met anyone like the people featured in the articles, but whoever and wherever they were, I wanted to be them. It didn't matter that many looked more like my parents than me, as long as they were enthused about being in a meaningful relationship with soil.

Inspired by Mr. Waddle's magazines, I began to collect every new piece of information about alternative gardening and farming I could get my hands on. Ads in the back of *Organic Gardening* led me to other sources, and to subscribe to *Mother Earth News*, a publication for homesteaders that began in 1970. When I read that John and Jane Shuttleworth had published from their farm such articles as "The Owner-Built Home," "Solar Energy," "The Plains Indian Tipi," and "Living High on $6500 a Year," I knew they were my people and I ordered all of the back issues I could afford that year with my summer wages. Soon I was connected by print to the burgeoning homesteading community and reading about self-reliance and rural skills for people heading back to the land. Many of the people in those articles were part of the alternative community I had gravitated toward through rock and roll. Ponytails and beards were common in their cartoon drawings.

Though I knew that people were moving away from farming, I was now learning about people who were trying to buck America's economic trends and head in the opposite direction. This community

I had joined on paper now made it okay for me to openly admit to friends and family that I wanted to be a farmer. I must have mentioned my newfound passion to someone who worked for our school newspaper, because one of the student reporters wrote an article depicting me as the back-to-nature hippie guy out in the Vo-Ag greenhouse, an anomaly that they found fascinating. I felt uncomfortable being singled out among the others in my class, but I posed for the picture and answered their questions nonetheless.

None of what I was learning was new to my grandparents. When I brought up ideas I'd gleaned, whether about a barn raising, rare-breed chickens, running a cider press, or even plumbing an old farmhouse, they (or someone they knew) had already done it, raised it, or made it. Kerosene lanterns? They had a few stored in the basement. Farming with horses? Grandpa had once used the horse collar, traces, and hames that were still hanging down in the barn. To my grandparents, "back-to-the-land" was the equivalent of getting back to how their parents did things, or even how they lived and worked when they first got married. I never pulled out an article in my magazines they couldn't expound upon. I never tired of asking them to.

The underlying assumption of some of the new, or newly revived, literature was that small-scale farming—often as small as five acres, as touted by Maurice G. Kains in *Five Acres and Independence*—was the answer to the world's social, economic, and environmental problems. Though I'd never lived in a city that I needed to escape from, I found myself in agreement. From the "Mother's Bookshelf" section at the back of *Mother Earth News*, I ordered Euell Gibbons's *Stalking the Wild Asparagus* and reprints of books on keeping bees, building chicken coops, and preserving food from the garden. I even bought Stephen Gaskin's *Hey Beatnik! This Is the Farm Book*, along with classics like Helen and Scott Nearing's *Living the Good Life*. By reading these books, my back-to-the-land dreams started to seem more concrete, more attainable.

For Christmas, I asked my parents for a butcher knife, a hand-saw and miter box, and a cast-iron frying pan. I frequented nearby antique stores and purchased discarded tools, which were plentiful and cheap because, as we have seen, so many mountain farms were dying out and their equipment seemed outmoded. Using the bedding plants that I raised in Mr. Waddle's class, I raised a garden in our neighbor's backyard. Then, with my dad's help—he was by then selling used cars on the side for extra income in Marion—I bought a 1960 Chevy pickup. Now all I needed was a farm!

With no savings or income to speak of, I knew I couldn't afford to buy Grandpa's place or any other farm in the family, even if someone were sympathetic enough to offer it to me. Yet, encouraged by the literature I'd become immersed in, I started to imagine that I could find an alternative way into agriculture. I asked Grandpa about mountain land prices, and he said that in places like Endicott where he had grown up, you could still find steep land for as little as five hundred dollars an acre, sometimes less. My creative wheels were cranking.

What if farming didn't need to provide for the trappings of my family's middle-class life? Did one really need new clothes, indoor plumbing, or electricity? What if I could learn to dovetail notch and trowel on concrete chinking, and build my own cabin? I already knew I could grow a small plot of food from seed. Maybe I could also grow strawberries and sell those for a little extra cash for gas, groceries, and other necessities. I imagined selling my paintings, too—I had sold one painting in a high school art show already! I could help reverse the tide of small farming's diminishment and my own family's tenure on the land. I could go back to the deep mountains where my ancestors first settled.

The Vo-Ag administrators could never have imagined it, but my unconventional turn toward farming was about to become a check mark on their charts of success. Though their work with rural youths probably had not increased the numbers of farmers in our county since the 1940s, the alternative farm movement I discovered through a stack of donated magazines in Mr. Waddle's office had made me an exception. Even as Secretary of Agriculture Butz was preaching across rural America that year that farmers should increase their acreage and invest in mechanization or leave farming altogether, I had decided somehow to get small and get in.

Before long, the idea of going back to the land began driving my academic interests, too. When my college-prep English teacher, Mr. Blankenship, asked each student in our class to choose a book and author to report on for the semester, Henry David Thoreau's *Walden* jumped out at me from the list he provided. I had seen copies of the classic for sale in "Mother's Bookshelf." Now I could read this book for a grade. I'm sure Mr. Blankenship was pleased that I volunteered to read anything at all.

Soon I was poring over the old frayed and taped copy of *Walden* from our high school library. Joining scores of 1970s back-to-the-landers, I was captivated by Thoreau's words of escape from the quiet desperation of mainstream society, of finding independence from economic restraints, and of satisfaction in his own hand labor. He convinced me that living the life one imagines in the woods was both possible and desirable, and his precise bookkeeping figures showed me that one could earn enough from the husbandry of two and a half acres of beans to pay one's bills. He taught me that the American back-to-the-land idea was well over a century old. I was nowhere near alone in my endeavor, and that gave me courage.

As I worked on my paper for class, I began copying Thoreau quotes to index cards and taping them to my bedroom wall. "Simplify, simplify," I wrote in large letters. I was especially drawn to the plan for Thoreau's ten-by-fifteen-foot hut that he built himself. I studied his meticulous lists of materials. I retraced the design of his living space on a sketch pad. I studied descriptions of his simple furniture. To me his lifestyle also represented a spiritual approach to nature and economics. He had been most practical, while also according his actions with the philosophical position that he, Ralph Waldo Emerson, and others called transcendentalism. Though I didn't understand everything he wrote, I swallowed it whole anyway.

The most important lesson *Walden* taught me was that speaking out against misguided American values was an old tradition. With Thoreau, I no longer felt alone in my American angst and disappointment. And he spoke to me directly, saying that heading into the woods to live was attainable in "common hours." I began dreaming of doing so even before I got a car. Nearly every painting I did in art class was of a cabin, replacing my earlier farmscapes. Building my own Thoreauvian structure became an obsession. "If you have built castles in the air, your work need not be lost," Thoreau wrote; "put the foundations under them." I believed him. The next time I saw Grandpa, I decided to ask him as earnestly as I knew how for a spot on which to build. "Do you have a place on your land somewhere that I could cut logs and build a cabin?"

I had some tools standing at the ready. With Grandpa's help with techniques, I was convinced we could fell trees and stack logs by hand. I would ask my cousin and other friends to help me notch and place the logs on rock pillars and then chink them. Of course, I wanted Grandpa to supervise, and he could decide where I would build. The only requirement was that the cabin needed to be near a spring, I said. And I would promise to take care not to make a mess. He was probably the only adult in my life I would have entrusted with what could have seemed an outlandish idea. He had certainly come through for me before.

Grandpa's answer did not disappoint. In fact, it stunned me. "I already have an old log cabin up in the mountain," he replied, explaining that an abandoned two-story house was still intact on some timberland he had bought some twenty-five miles away. "It's up near Shooting Creek," he said. I knew that this couldn't be far from where his family had eked out a living. I was speechless.

He continued: "There's a waterfall up there named Raven's Den, and the trees ought to be getting up pretty good in size." He had purchased the land and cut only the largest timber off the place ten years earlier and left the rest to grow. There were nearly 350 acres there, he said. I vaguely remembered going with him to haul logs from the site when I was six years old.

"The last time I saw that cabin, it was still in good shape," he explained. "It was two stories, with two rock chimneys, and was made from big hand-cut logs about yea high," he added, holding his hands about eighteen inches apart. "We just have to wait until the snakes go in their holes for the winter. But I'll go up there with you. If the cabin's still there, you could fix that place up instead of building something from the ground up. It would be a lot easier."

I couldn't believe my good fortune. I called my cousin Bruce right away and asked him to join us in the endeavor. After we talked, the wait of two or three months seemed interminable. We finally got a chance to go and see the place on a crisp November day. The cabin we found was an old two-story log farmhouse covered with milled wood siding. It had two beautiful hand-laid rock chimneys, all stacked by masons who had used no mortar. The place was a work of art. The one-story kitchen built off the back was still in good shape, but vines nearly covered the front of the place, and the roof had rotted through on the main part of the cabin, leaving most of the wooden shakes from the front roof in a pile on the interior floor. Despite some superficial damage, somehow the floor was still mostly intact. The "bones" remained strong even if the exterior looked rough. We had found the place barely in time. There was no doubt that I had to adopt it.

A few weeks later Grandpa, Bruce, and I began laying cheap roll roofing over the last of the rotting wood shingles to save the floor below before winter set in. We could barely hold on to roofing nails while hanging upside down by our feet, as Grandpa shouted instructions from below. "Boys, don't waste them nails," he pleaded as one nail after another escaped our grasp and went rolling off the edge. We could see him stoop to pick each one up off the ground and place them back in the paper bag he held. Knowing how frugal he was, we felt chagrined at our ineptitude. We wanted him to know we weren't being careless; we were doing the best we knew how. Even if we were laughing at our lack of ability, we took the job seriously. We eventually did prevail—two teenagers only sixteen and fifteen when we started—putting on a roof that would last for years. We had begun teaching ourselves carpentry and other homesteading skills, with our own grandfather helping when he could. Years later, Bruce would start his own construction company.

The cabin was almost impossible to access by two-wheel drive, and my sluggish old pickup was particularly unsuited for the task. So we carried most all of our groceries and building supplies in by hand. It had no plumbing or electricity, smelled of old grease and smoke, and was infested with pack rats. It was dark and all the windows had been broken out. Despite that, I loved the place and began sinking all my spare money and free time into making the house my imagined home.

Then I informed my parents that I planned to move there—well before finishing high school—and Bruce decided he would do so as well. We could enroll in the local county high school and make money by selling my paintings and working for local farmers and contractors. I fantasized that I could also sell local strawberries, which one of my farming books touted as a homesteader's best moneymaker. Though thankfully we had freedom to go to the cabin anytime we wanted, our parents squelched the unsupervised high school idea, saying, "Why don't you finish high school, get your college degree, and then you can move up there."

Though disappointed, I accepted their advice.

The Woolwine "cabin" as we found it in 1973.

Pruning | *1974*

*W*hen I first began thumbtacking Thoreau's quotes up around the cabin walls, I believed my every aspiration paralleled his. As far as I knew, I *was* going "confidently in the direction of [my] dreams." I was, in fact, striving to "live the life I had imagined." I spent every extra dollar I had to make this new life a reality. My relatives helped by buying paint, making curtains, and sending food. Grandma let me have her parents' kerosene lamps, two old iron bedsteads, and some dishes. Though, of course, the land still belonged to my grandparents, they said we could use the place as long as they could hold on to it. At first, I didn't stop to ponder what that last caveat might mean, so I continued going there for years to come, until they could no longer pay the taxes on the land. Selling the mountain land would become one of their strategies for holding on to the farm where they lived.

Though Bruce and other family and friends often accompanied me, I regularly went to the cabin alone, including for several one- and two-week stays. That seemed like such a long time to me that I put up a mailbox and registered with the post office. Then to the best of my ability, I acted as if I were self-reliant. I fished for trout, stalked the wild asparagus as Euell Gibbons had taught, and picked wineberries and blackberries with which I made turnovers and cobblers. I prepared everything I ate on an old wood-burning cook stove I bought for twenty dollars. I had learned to bake biscuits and cornbread and a variety of different dishes from my grandmother, though pork and beans and canned spaghetti were also common fare. I heated creek water in the stove's reservoir for washing dishes and taking sponge baths. The kerosene lamps provided light to cook and read by at night. As far as I knew how, I pared down to the "essential facts of life."

While staying at the cabin, I came to learn some hard facts that I hadn't planned on, including how different my circumstances were from Thoreau's. He was twenty-seven when he began his experiment; eleven years older than I was when I started. He had completed a degree at Harvard College, learned to read in more than five languages, and started his own private school, all before he went to the woods. I hadn't yet graduated from Marion Senior High. He helped run his family's pencil-making business, published numerous works of poetry and prose, and was fairly established economically when he began building his house. I had only worked part-time in a factory and a state park in Marion, and I had put aside nothing. During my time in the woods, I only composed letters to my girlfriend and wrote thoughts to myself in a spiral notebook. It is obvious how that compares with Thoreau's thousands of published pages, many of them about his sojourn at Walden Pond. When Thoreau boasted that during his two years he maintained himself "solely by the labour of my hands," of course I was deeply impressed. But I also began to understand that one never really lives solely on one's own. One's background and circumstances can mean everything, such that when we venture out supposedly on our own, we carry with us a village, and the village and its assets support us even when we live apart from it. For example, Thoreau never purchased the land he lived on at Walden Pond. Not everyone can come by such privilege, no matter how hard they might try.

I also realized how different Thoreau's village of Concord must have been from the Blue Ridge hollows of Woolwine where the first occupants built our cabin. Our old, drafty place, even by the time we found it in the late 1970s, was still three miles from the closest state road. Its structure, while sturdy, recalled a life when farmers with very little income had to make do with what they could fashion by hand, raise, or trade for. Everyone lived by their own labor when the place was built, and many inhabitants of the southern Blue Ridge continued to live that way past World War II, a century after

Thoreau left the woods so he could live "more lives." In other words, when it was built, the old cabin in Woolwine represented not an alternative lifestyle, but the only form of local life possible then, a hardscrabble existence from birth to death. For most, to leave that backwoods life meant going far away or dying. And yet there I was, returning by choice to an existence lived by previous generations out of necessity. I was like Thoreau in that I paid nothing for the land I used when I went to the woods, but so different from him in many other ways.

In 1845, sixteen years before start of the Civil War, Thoreau borrowed an axe from his friend Bronson Alcott and removed himself from society's influences in order to live "free and clear for study." Even as he did so, however, he remained at the center of American intellectual life. The cabin he built at Walden Pond on Ralph Waldo Emerson's property allowed him to meet with Emerson and his followers regularly, along with other literati, including the Alcotts, the Hawthorns, Thomas Carlyle, the poet Ellery Channing, and others. His writing had a ready audience and he entertained many visitors who were eager to engage with him. When he walked to town, as he often did, the trip took him no more than an hour even when stopping to bird-watch. The walk to have his mother and sister do his laundry was shorter than that, at only twenty minutes. He had a hot meal and a bath whenever he needed them.

From its inception, our cabin had existed on an American periphery, where, as we have seen, the inhabitants had no education, health care, or infrastructure to call upon. No factories were built nearby, not even a simple one that made pencils. There were sawmills and gristmills turned by water, and even a few legal distilleries, but those provided only a few jobs. Though some local youths left for the coalfields when mining began, the majority of the region's inhabitants were subsistence farmers, though some became part-time store owners, millers, coopers, and carpenters on the side. Even during my time there, our cabin was still twenty miles from the nearest library. A walk to town would have taken all day. The drive to Grandpa's, the closest place to shower, took me thirty minutes in my pickup.

A literary community, mine was not. The letters I wrote and mailed mainly to my girlfriend could sometimes border on philosophical reflections, but those missives were never more than thoughts written by a teenager with no scholarly training. And my musings never led me to interlocutions with anyone who might have engaged in conversation about transcendentalism or the immorality of American slavery, topics that held Thoreau's attention. One somewhat sophisticated aunt who had married into our family had once said about me, "He marches to a different drummer," recalling Thoreau. Yet, quite unlike Thoreau, no one ever asked me to describe my drummer's cadence. No one ever talked with me about why I felt drawn to the woods. I had to figure that out on my own.

As I explored our cabin's surroundings, I learned the community had begun to break up when great numbers of mountain youths left home to serve in the two world wars. Others left for textile and furniture factories in towns like Spray, North Carolina, and Stuart, Martinsville, Bassett, Danville, and Newport News, Virginia. Other rivulets of migrants flowed out of Woolwine and joined the great mountain streams of exodus of the mid-twentieth century, most of them heading to northern manufacturing centers like Baltimore, Philadelphia, and even Chicago. With the young living—and often dying—elsewhere, the old generation left at home tended their land as best they could on their own. As with many migrants working in the United States today, mountain migrants who found work away sent money back to help their parents, and returned home when they could. But few came back home to live. As a result, by the 1970s the centuries-long tenure on most mountain farms was ending. Like our family's places in Endicott, the old Woolwine place had also been a farm, though by the time Grandpa bought the land in the early 1960s in an estate sale, the farm fields had grown back into an impressive stand of timber. Cleared mountain fields seen in photographs from the 1930s already looked to the uninitiated as if they had never been cut. Grandpa's cabin, like all the ramshackle homes in Shooting Creek that I passed by growing up, was one of the last remaining sentinels pointing back to the region's self-reliant, agricultural past.

Some of the last living self-reliant people of the North Georgia mountains, quite similar to those anywhere in Appalachia, were profiled in the Foxfire book series by Eliot Wigginton and his students in Rabun Gap, Georgia. Fascinated by the subjects, I bought the first volume soon after it came out in 1972, along with several of the volumes that followed. Wigginton's students in Georgia were kindred spirits, and their celebration of Appalachian mountain culture gave me a renewed sense of purpose in preserving the knowledge of the old homesteaders living near our cabin. The books also served as a welcome antidote to prejudices against mountain people that I heard even from some in my high school. For anyone who said mountain people are just dumb hillbillies, the Foxfire books showed in detail Appalachian brilliance, resourcefulness, creativity, and strong will. Most important, they showed that some mountain people still practiced skills now being "rediscovered" by *Mother Earth News* readers and other homesteaders. The past wasn't past after all, they proved.

Mimicking the Foxfire style, I asked my elderly neighbors nearby the cabin about fruit and vegetable growing, firewood, springhouses, and even sawmilling and grain grinding with waterpower. Now that their children had moved away and their grandchildren were growing up elsewhere, they welcomed me—a curious teenager who appreciated what they remembered and who wanted to listen to their stories. Luckily, when I lived at the cabin I had the time to visit and I needed the company. My neighbors told me of life not so long before when everyone lived without electricity and cars. They remembered when people used to walk dirt paths between houses and send messages by farm bells. "People had time for each other back then," they said. "Now, everyone's too busy to sit and talk." I was one person doing my part to reverse that trend.

One such neighbor named Roy DeHart was a font of information about the community as it had been. Most important, he remembered the McAlexanders who had last owned and lived in our old cabin. They raised a family there, he said, but the parents grew old and lived alone in the house in their final years.

"They raised everything they ate," he said. "And they lived fairly well as long as they could work. But then they got sick and couldn't work. When they died, the house just sat up there lonely, no one came back to tend it." Then came this surprise: "Old Man Asa's grave is right up there in the woods up on a ridge in front of the house," he said. As there was no road or path to it, I had no clue to its whereabouts. After Mr. DeHart told me, the very next day I hiked up to the narrow hilltop to where Asa had dug his own grave, and the returning children and their neighbors had carried the casket and buried him under a hemlock tree by hand. Standing at the granite marker they placed on the grave, I pondered Asa's life.

Mr. DeHart had told me Mr. McAlexander, like many of his neighbors, made whiskey to sell. "It was the only way to make a dollar back in them days," he said. On one of our excursions, Bruce and I discovered a rusted sheet metal submarine moonshine still beside the small creek that babbled several hundred yards from the house. The still had been gashed by axes and was left where lawmen had demolished it. People told me that if a bootlegger knew the law was on the way—often warned by a neighbor's bell—he would grab the copper cap and worm, and then run for the woods. People could remake the rock and sheet metal parts, but the store-bought copper was the most expensive and hardest to replace. The shell of the still was but one remnant of the McAlexanders who had owned it.

In addition to fixing up the old house, Bruce and I rebuilt the old McAlexander springhouse, and also attempted to get the corncrib in working order. But as we tried to clean up around the log barn by burning the brush around it, the fire got away from us and we accidentally burned down the entire structure. We sweated for hours fighting the brushfire with hand tools and buckets of creek water, but lost the battle in the end. Even after working on such projects for twelve-hour days, we knew we barely made a dent in reclaiming the place. We came to marvel at the amazing work of the farmers who, without power tools, electricity, or running water, built the homestead. Of course they didn't just dabble or experiment in rural living. For mountain farmers, the options were to grow, build, and make their necessities, or die.

Living and working on their old farm, the McAlexanders gradually came to life for me, though this resurrection wasn't always a comfort. "Old Man Asa would climb high up into the trees and preach . . . to the squirrels!" Mr. DeHart told me. I imagined a man expounding on scripture with a preacher's shout echoing off the hillsides. Was he calling to the heavens, a literal voice crying in the wilderness, or was he raging against loneliness he experienced at the end of his life? Would visits and medical care have helped him? Another neighbor told me that Asa's wife, Callie, carried a loaded revolver under a cloth in her egg basket as she traveled up the mountain path to the local store. She wasn't to be messed with, they said. The same neighbor also told me she set the whole mountain on fire to rid it of snakes. Was that rumor true? If the McAlexanders were scared, was the real villain the isolation that moved in after their children had gone? Would things have worked out differently if the economy had provided jobs so the children could stay nearby? Those were the kinds of questions I pondered while falling asleep alone at night in the McAlexanders' home in my grandparents' creaky iron bed. With my dog Betsy to keep me company, I learned to quiet my fears, accept the spirits of the past, and listen—sometimes amid the howling winds that could sound a lot like human cries—for what the remnants of their lives might teach me.

As I listened, my whole perspective about self-reliance changed. I began to think about how when people get old and too frail to work, Thoreau-like solitude doesn't look so romantic anymore. Living by my own ingenuity for voluntary stretches as a teenage, part-time homesteader was one thing; the isolation of the last remaining generation grown old and frail on a farm that yielded no cash was another. I went to the woods with Thoreau, thinking I would learn how to live on my own, and I learned plenty; but I also traversed a topography of poverty. I fell in love with woods, trout streams, and waterfalls, and I learned a little about how to live without running water and electricity; but I also entered another America, a land of the not-so-free to live life as they had imagined it.

Walden gave me a road map to follow when I most needed one; I celebrated mountain ingenuity with Foxfire; and I dreamed of rekindling the best of America with the authors of *Mother Earth News*. But none of that prepared me to think about the realities of economic marginalization where deprivation, unlike simplicity, is not exactly something to celebrate. I discovered that, in fact, some people cannot merely advance in the direction they choose. I started to learn that the stereotypes about the rural mountain poor being shiftless and lazy I had heard and seen so many times, from *Hee Haw* and *The Beverly Hillbillies* on TV to *Li'l Abner* and *Barney Google and Snuffy Smith* in the comics, came from outsider prejudice that made light of the real problems that mountain people faced and gave them no credit for their inventiveness in the face of hardship. Above all, I started to realize these mountaineers were my people, and that I wanted to learn more about our collective past.

I knew this much from experience already: One can't live on one's own and apart from the cash economy without being intelligent and a hard worker, which is why when Grandma said someone was "smart," she meant not only astute, but also industrious. In the mountains where Callie and Asa McAlexander and their neighbors built their own homes with neighbors' help, there was no separating the work of one's head from that of their hands, or one's success from the help of family and neighbors. People survived because they were resourceful and cooperative in spite of being bypassed by economic advancement elsewhere. I started to understand rural poverty as a social ill and not as an individual fault, and I saw how people invented home remedies to address this illness: They became self-sufficient, not as an experiment or as a means of rejecting society, but as a survival strategy.

Ted Boyd (banjo) and his band from Ferrum, Virginia playing at the Blue Ridge Folklife Festival in 1979. Photo courtesy of the Blue Ridge Institute & Museum of Ferrum College.

Transplanting | *1975*

*A*s I drove out of our driveway in Marion and headed to college alone, I understood my education was only possible because my parents had been among the mountain generation who left farms for manufacturing jobs. I knew federal grants and loans would help me with my education, along with funds I had saved by working summers and after school. Later I found work as a janitor at an elementary school. But my parents' work had provided my freedom to simply drive away.

I hadn't yet ranged far from home in my travels, but I had gone deep enough into my region to understand the advantage of education. As if to accentuate the two main pathways open to us in Marion, my best friend in high school, Dennis, stayed behind hoping to climb the economic ladder through factory work. He had started out as a night watchman and was now moving toward a daytime supervisory role. He believed in the stability of the factories, and that if he worked hard, like his father, he would get promotions and move up by his own wits. He was not alone. Of our small graduating class of 175, only a small fraction of us would go on to complete four-year degrees. No one had to remind me of the privilege of driving away with no plan to return.

I was headed to Ferrum College, in part because it was nestled in the Blue Ridge twenty-five miles from the cabin, but mostly because it was one of the few colleges I had ever seen up close. Ferrum was first established in 1913 as a mission of the Methodist Church, just like my grandfather's little elementary school in Endicott, but on a larger scale and for upper grades.

My grandmother, whose family had a few more resources than my grandfather's, drove herself to high school there. A generation later, my father earned his associate's degree there in the junior college it became. By the time I headed to Ferrum in 1975, it had grown into a four-year college. Though I didn't know it when I applied, it was still considered a mission school of sorts, one that served primarily first-generation college students. Though on the Thompson side I was just that, what I considered the biggest draw was its location just three miles from my grandparents' farm. Going to college there meant I could live with my favorite people year-round.

The plan our family worked out was that I would attend the college as a day student, and live and work with Grandma and Grandpa in exchange for room and board. I would major in art, work on their farm, and continue to fix up the old cabin in my spare time. I loaded all my clothes, books, magazines, tools, and many of the houseplants I'd grown in Mr. Waddle's horticulture class into the back of the Econoline van, for which my dad had helped me trade the Chevy truck.

I headed toward Interstate 81 with an eight-track copy of Neil Young's *Harvest* playing on my stereo, singing "Old man take a look at my life, I'm a lot like you" in falsetto at the top of my lungs. The Marion on-ramp led to a steep uphill climb. Putting the automatic transmission in low, I floored the gas pedal and waited for the engine to slowly build up torque. But even at the van's highest rpm, it still sounded sick. I was still doing only forty-five when I swerved left into traffic, avoiding the tractor trailer passing me. With the gas pedal still pressed to the floor, I only drove another few hundred feet before I noticed flashing blue lights in my rearview mirror. I pulled over and waited for the trooper to approach the driver's-side window. I could see him checking out the contents of the van through the windows as he walked toward me.

As he walked up to my window and asked for my license, he was still checking out the back of the van. His next question was not about my speeding, as is usually the case with teenage drivers, but rather, "Do you know how slow you were going?" It was an embarrassing moment for an eighteen-year-old. I explained my van's lack of power, especially when loaded down with all my possessions. No one could have gone faster up that hill in this van. Keeping his poker face, the trooper returned to his car and let me wait. Then mercifully he brought back a yellow slip of paper and said he was letting me go with a warning. He and I both knew I could have gotten a ticket for slow driving that I could never live down. I learned later that Trooper Gilmore knew my father from his used-car lot. He told my dad that he'd seen the plants leaning against the rear window of the van and thought he had nabbed a pot dealer.

In the mid-1970s, Ferrum College began embracing its mountain heritage and promoting itself as a destination where one could study Blue Ridge culture, which was great news for my college experience. Its new emphasis on mountain traditions gave the institution, which was otherwise unknown to most students outside the region, a much-needed boost of new applicants. During my freshman year, director Roddy Moore's Blue Ridge Institute, a newly funded center for the study of traditional folk culture, started the Blue Ridge Folklife Festival. It featured mountain arts and crafts, and included demonstrations of dozens of mountain skills from coon dog hunting and liquor distilling (using water for demonstration purposes) to cooking Brunswick stew and making music, from church shape-note singing to bluegrass and blues. Two centerpieces of the college campus became two model farmsteads that represented agriculture in the 1800s and the early 1900s, with students serving as guides.

In my freshman year, Grandpa and I attended Ferrum's first folk festival together. Soon after we arrived, he heard string band music playing under a big tent. He pulled me out on the dance floor—really just a few sheets of reinforced plywood laid out on the grass—where we "cut a rug" together. I had learned some mountain flatfoot dancing a few years earlier at a fiddlers' convention. When I acted surprised at how good he was, he told me that he danced when he was a boy, though he hadn't gone to dances since he'd been married. I had also started learning traditional music on the fiddle and mandolin while in Marion, never knowing that Grandpa's history with old-time and blue-grass music went much beyond what he listened to on television, like the programs featuring Flatt and Scruggs, and Jim & Jesse. Seeing how much he enjoyed dancing showed me that this had been his music and culture long before TV, and certainly long before I "discovered" it. I had found even more traits to admire in Grandpa, and dancing to the string band with him also taught me that though elements of our unique culture seemed to skip a generation, it was still alive.

With my interest in traditional culture now paramount, I enrolled in art classes in the same building where my father had attended elementary school, which was now owned by the college. One art classroom was filled with old tools that we studied for inspiration. In addition to art classes, I also chose a Blue Ridge folkways project for my freshman English course. When I asked Grandma for help finding an interviewee to work with, she phoned Mrs. Young—the oldest woman in the community, who seemed to know everyone—to see if she knew of anyone "keeping the old traditions" in Ferrum. Mrs. Young recommended the Kesslers, an elderly brother and sister who lived not far from the college on their old family farm up an isolated dirt road. "They live the old way and cook and heat with wood," she said. Then she added, "But they are pretty old themselves, and they might need some help." The Kesslers had no phone, but Mrs. Young said I should just drive in to see them when the opportunity arose. She would mention me to them sometime if she saw them.

A few weeks later, I drove up their curvy and rutted dirt road leading through the woods; when I reached the clearing around the house, I got out, walked up to the house, and knocked. Ms. Pearl Kessler came to the door and welcomed me in, apologizing for how old the house looked, though I noticed right away there was a parlor of sorts off to the right where fancy red stuffed chairs were covered in plastic and sat unused. That room was their sole nod to middle-class living in a house that otherwise needed attention. We then entered the kitchen where she introduced me to her brother John, who was bedridden in a single bed in the corner. Soon I realized he couldn't enunciate his words, but made mumbling sounds that told me he knew I was there.

Ms. Kessler was literally her brother's keeper. Being unmarried and without children, they had no one around to check on them during the day. A nephew and his wife who lived nearby helped as much as possible, but they worked away from home. It was obvious there were no resources to pay anyone. Not knowing what else I might do, I started splitting firewood and kindling, mowing their yard, or cleaning up around the place each time I visited. When I went into the house after working, I agreed, at Ms. Kessler's behest, to read the Bible to them before we ate a meal together. Once, Mr. Kessler began to sob audibly as I read a passage. His loud display of emotion gave me pause at first, but with Ms. Kessler's nod, I continued, reading through his crying, trying to concentrate on the words and not on my own feeling of helplessness. Perhaps the reading was a comfort to the Kesslers on some level, but inside I knew that, when I finished, nothing had changed.

Though I was never satisfied that I had done enough for the Kesslers, they taught me a great deal, just as Mrs. Young had predicted they would—not so much about traditional skills celebrated in the mountain cultural revival, but about life itself. Foremost, they gave me a jolt of realization that the life of isolation the McAlexanders lived in their last years was still very much extant in the 1970s. The Kesslers were not some anachronistic holdovers from the past who chose to live without conveniences, and to now serve as the objects of study for students. Rather, they were hardworking old farm people whom society had cast aside as it "progressed." They were the creations of the changes wrought by the economy, not outliers who dropped out of it. As the last of their generation still hanging on to their land and trying to survive, the Kesslers now were forced to live out their years alone and without support. With surrounding community members now gone elsewhere to find wage work in factories and larger cities, they were barely surviving as the old style of community reliance became obsolete. Selling the land would have been their only recourse, but they were too old to leave and had no place to go. Their nephew who lived away from the community later told me they had saved old coins that were of some value and maybe those could have helped, but someone had robbed them only a short while before I arrived. Mr. and Mrs. Young were later robbed, too, by two men who said they were selling rugs. One held up rugs as if on display, while the other went behind the rugs and rummaged through drawers in the other room. Having no younger family members around to care for them as in generations past, the old people became targets.

I saw how badly these people needed help, and as a result, my eighteen-year-old interests and offerings in return now mortified me. I dropped the idea of asking the Kesslers about folk crafts altogether, but continued going to see them for the rest of the semester. I never even mentioned my "project." Instead, for my class I carved a wooden spoon out of some scrap lumber I found, and made a mallet from a dogwood branch that I cut at Grandpa's, and I turned those in for part of my grade. I also learned an old church ballad that I sang in class, "Shake Hands with Mother Again," that bespoke a land beyond suffering where departures and good-byes are no more. It seemed a fitting tribute to the Kesslers. But I never mentioned the family to my professor even though they remained on my mind as I performed the song in class.

One cold December day a month or so later, as I drove to the college for one of my last morning New Testament classes—a requirement for all Ferrum students—the Kesslers suddenly came to my mind again in association with Matthew 25:40, which I'd just read: "Verily I say unto you, inasmuch as ye have done it unto one of the least of these my brethren, ye have done it unto me." This gave me pause. Instead of grabbing my books and rushing into the classroom, I found myself sitting in the day student parking lot in my van, staring at the dashboard, wondering what to do. Though class would be starting a few minutes later, I finally decided I had to go to the Kesslers' home. "I'm doing well in the course," I said aloud as I restarted the engine, raced through the college exit, and drove as fast as the van would take me toward their dirt road. When I arrived some twenty minutes later and knocked, Ms. Kessler met me at the door crying, saying, "I'm so thankful you came." She guided me back into the familiar main room, where I found that Mr. Kessler had fallen out of bed and had been lying on the drafty floor for hours. He was also crying loudly. His sister had only been able to cover him up with blankets where he lay. They had had no means to call for help. Somehow her cries seemed to have reached me anyway. I lifted Mr. Kessler's frail body into the bed and helped her cover him. I don't know how long he would have lain on the floor had I not come along.

That day I began to realize that living in the woods, growing food, and making art for a living was no longer enough for me. I had seen the fabric of rural life tearing apart. I had seen firsthand how irrelevant the self-reliant, pull-yourself-up-by-the-bootstraps dream was when it came to the Kesslers. In fact, it was a lie. Without community support, economic development, and health care for the needy, life in the mountains, or any other place for that matter, simply cannot sustain itself. Coming face-to-face with these sad realities made me rethink everything about the mountains. Instead of heading to the woods, I decided I had to do something about the rural decline I was witnessing. I had no idea how, but I knew I needed to change my educational focus.

I avoided mentioning anything to my grandparents for fear they would think they had somehow played a role in my change of heart. All I knew to do was to take a walk in the woods and think about all this alone. Later I spent time in the college library looking at catalogs from other colleges in our region, hoping to find some way to address our rural social problems. Of the ones

I picked up in the library's small assortment—how random a research strategy that seems now—the curriculum of Emory & Henry College spoke to me loudest. Also nestled in the Virginia mountains, just some twenty-five miles from Marion, Emory & Henry's materials said their curriculum emphasized community service. That language clicked. That students could make a difference in the world was the message I needed.

Without saying anything to my family, I wrote to the E&H admissions office to apply for a transfer of my credits. I knew that going there would mean that all my drawing and painting classes would count only as electives. If I were to graduate in four years, I could take no more art. I would have to put aside my canvases and paintbrushes. I didn't want to admit it at first, but I also knew somehow that going there would probably mean giving up on living permanently in the old cabin as well.

Most heart wrenching of all, transferring would mean leaving the farm and my grandparents. I knew that telling Grandma, who was by then suffering from rheumatoid arthritis and unable to cook most meals, would be the hardest. When I received the letter of acceptance, I had to build up my nerve for days before talking to them. Sitting with them in their den, I told them I felt pulled to work with poor people, and this meant finding a different major; after pausing a few seconds, I blurted out, "and transferring to a different school." Grandma listened patiently, but as soon as I finished, she immediately apologized that she hadn't done a better job with cooking. I was stricken. I knew she had worked hard all her life to make her home perfect, and that Grandpa had taken over many of the kitchen and housecleaning chores when she could no longer do them. How could I convince her that her health had nothing to do with my decision to change schools? "Please, Grandma," I said, choking back tears as I tried to tell her how much I appreciated her support and loved being on the farm. Then I tried to explain why I needed to be more engaged in the world. Since I didn't quite yet understand all of it myself, I'm sure I did a pathetic job of describing the change coming over me. Though she accepted my words with grace, I was never satisfied with them.

I could have easily stayed with Grandma and Grandpa for the remaining three years of my college life. I could have cared for them and their land just as they had cared for me. Yet, paradoxically, there I was deciding to leave while at the same time voicing that my goal was to help rural people. My commitments birthed on that farm were thus pulling me away from those I loved the most. My heart felt as though it were tearing in two.

But of course the rending of a single heart is not the whole story, for in reality my decision was society's as a whole. Macroeconomics had made many of my farming choices for me, rendering my life decisions in ways that cannot be explained by individual resolve, a sense of calling, or a choice of college curriculum. Pulling back to view the larger picture, we see a family succumbing to the realities of agricultural concentration with no choice of farm succession plans. Grandpa made so little money from his farm then that there would have been no way for me to work with him for a living. Even remaining as his paid helper was impossible. Such realities were unrelated to his work ethic and management ability, and even to my commitment to agriculture, but instead were the result of our nation's choices in farm policies that dictated the raw numbers of farm finances. In short, my decision was not mine alone. Staying longer on the farm as a student would have prolonged my bliss, but working hard would have done nothing to help me support myself as an adult. My work would have taken me not a step closer to being a farmer.

Though I had mentioned to my family that we could try raising pick-your-own strawberries and blueberries to supplement the beef cattle—ideas I had gleaned from my reading the new farm press—there was no way I could have found the money to prove that a new plan could work. If some entity had given me a grant or loan, I probably would have taken over the farm straightaway. But I had no collateral, and I had no chance to make a down payment. When I hinted that we might consider family financing, my father said he didn't want to saddle me with that kind of debt. He wouldn't have wanted to cosign on a loan with me either, especially because interest rates were in the teens then. Besides, I wasn't even twenty years old at the time, so how could the family believe I was ready to shoulder the responsibility of running a farm? I had some money saved from my various jobs, but nowhere near enough to buy even a few acres of mountain land and Grandpa's cabin, let alone take over 150 acres of improved farmland, a farmhouse, and all the outbuildings. So I was forced to accept the fact that the last chapter of our farm story would soon end, and that there was nothing I could do about it.

I had tried to hold on to agriculture by exploring ways of going back to the land, but instead of finding answers I witnessed poor people living in isolation in the aftermath of the loss of rural communities. I now knew "the land" was not the source of utopia it had once seemed. Instead I started to grasp that everything about rural life in America was interconnected with politics controlled elsewhere. So I reformulated my goals into a commitment to give back to rural areas in some general way, and in the long run to work to change society. Hence, my budding decision to work in the field that I came to call "rural justice" grew directly from our family losing its farm. This occupation would not be the same as farming on my own, but at least preparing for that work would give my next years in college a deep significance as I tried to make sense of the losses on my closest horizon.

★ ★ ★

Years later, Grandma lay in a hospital in a coma. As the family gathered in the waiting room, I entered her room alone and spoke to her motionless body. "Grandma, if you can hear me, I want you to know that I always loved staying with you so much. I'm so grateful for all that you did for us. I loved your cooking, but I know that you couldn't get up in the mornings because of your pain. Please understand that I did not leave Ferrum College because you couldn't provide enough for me. You have done everything you could for me throughout my life, and I want to thank you for all your love and sacrifice. I want you to know that I do my work because of you." Then I placed my hand on her left foot that was poking out of the covers and said, "If you can hear me, please move your toes." Her foot flickered to life, and her toes bent twice.

At the Siler City, North Carolina, livestock auction, 1986. Photograph by Rob Amberg.

Gleaning | *1976*

*A*s the places where I felt most comfortable started to give way beneath me, I grasped for the spiritual. First, I turned to the Baptist faith with which I had been raised. I began searching for congregations and reading the Bible in earnest. I didn't find a church that fit well, but I was gratified to discover Bible stories that helped me interpret my experiences with the land and people in our region. The greatest surprise was what I had presumed to be spiritual explorations in fact began to undergird my concerns about material problems in the modern world. The stories spoke directly about present predicaments.

Reading the Garden of Eden story, for example, I received it as a tale of people living with family and their subsequent story of exile, struggle, and death. I interpreted the Hebrews' forty-year search for land as a period of yearning for would-be farmers; a landless and formerly enslaved people wandering in the desert dreaming of a land of milk and honey where they could tend cattle, plant olive trees, and eat what they produce. Though I was uncomfortable with their wars against enemies over land, their story taught me that people really do fight and die over territory, and how refugees displaced by wars have long been central to the human story.

The Jesus I found in the New Testament was a landless wanderer as well. When he bade his disciples to follow him, he told them they would be homeless, and that they would minister to those who could not help themselves—the sick, widows, and orphans—generally the outcasts of society. He had been born a refugee while his family was on the run. Despite his family's poverty, however, Jesus's teachings were filled with images of agriculture. His parables employed metaphors about food, seeds, and farm animals. His story of the Prodigal Son, for example, was about a wayward man who had left his father's farm, wasted his inheritance, and now was willing to return and live with the family's pigs. The main point was that many youths go away in search of themselves only to learn that a deeper relationship to family and land is what they sought all along. Though I was no inheritor of a farm and had renounced nothing, I nonetheless knew something about the loss of a future in farming.

Indignant about such losses, I found myself drawn to the biblical prophets who railed against hypocrisy and decried their society's oppression of the poor. I took their critiques at face value, as denunciations of societal inequality and actual suffering of its victims, just as I believed that Jesus was speaking literally about real poor people. I began to have an inkling why so many people like him became martyrs—they spoke truth to power.

These represent some of the thoughts that had begun churning through my head when I wrote my personal statement on the entrance forms for Emory & Henry, and why, when I got there, I declared religion as a major. I thought maybe I could find answers related to justice in that department. I added sociology and anthropology as a second major because I wanted to understand why our society had failed its rural poor. More than anything, I wanted to know why farms were failing, and what we could do about it.

Emory & Henry College, like Ferrum, also began as a mountain mission school with roots in the Methodist Church, and it continued into its second century with strong church connections. That meant that in religion classes I found myself surrounded by solid, church-trained students on their way to becoming preachers and Christian educators. They were smart people who had done well in their high schools, but most were steeped in a suburban status quo that I had rejected before leaving for college. I knew their kind of church career was not for me. The students in my sociology and anthropology classes were all decent people seeking careers in law, teaching, or social work. They cared about helping people, but much of the curriculum we studied was more focused on forging careers than on changing the world. I felt out of place. I started to wonder if I'd made a terrible mistake.

Part of me now wishes someone had told me that there were other colleges filled with activists engaged in the world around them, even colleges where one can work on a farm to help pay tuition, like Berea College in Kentucky and Warren Wilson College in North Carolina. At the same time, I knew it was essential for me to study close to home before moving on. Before I could do anything else, I first had to face the tenets of the faith with which I was raised. And I had to understand the socioeconomic challenges of the Virginia mountains while at E&H. Leaving could have been one way to reconstruct a life, but staying and being forced to dig deep to find answers about my origins would give me a greater sense of myself in my own vernacular.

I studied more during my first semester of my sophomore year than in all of my previous years in school put together, so much so that at first I had little free time to think about vocation or even to get outside. When, finally, I did well on a midterm paper in my most challenging class, I gave myself some breathing room to explore. I started taking hikes, and I began to keep a journal. With time for reflection, it became readily apparent, again, that I could not follow a route laid out by others. "Listen for your inner voice," I wrote in my journal. Before long, that voice would send me back to farming communities.

Fortunately, a few professors understood my desire to go beyond the classroom. With the help of sociologist Doug Boyce, I began volunteering with the local Community Action Program called People, Inc. My work there yielded an academic paper and confidence that fieldwork and community service were legitimate academic endeavors. More important, I also met people there who were engaged in community service as a vocation.

Through the People, Inc. director, I heard about the Brumley Gap campaign through which citizens were fighting to save their land from an ill-conceived dam that threatened to flood a whole valley filled with homes and small farms; this was my first exposure to an organized rural community fighting for survival. Inspired by their efforts, I read Si Kahn's *How People Get Power* and related books about social activism, and before long I turned my sociology and anthropology major into a self-designed concentration on community organizing.

While at People, Inc., I also learned that two of Emory's own political science professors, Steve Fisher and Jim Foster, were working with the citizens of Brumley Gap. Finding them together in the college administration building one afternoon, I asked them how I might get more involved in the organizing effort. They invited me to attend a benefit concert for Brumley Gap at the famous Carter Family Fold that Friday, and offered me a ride. At the Fold, they introduced me to Kathy and Rees Sheerer, full-time community organizers who lived on a small farm near Emory. They looked to be the type I'd read about in *Mother Earth News*, but they were also politically active in the communities around them. I told them I was interested in community organizing and later they invited me over for a meal.

Older than me by ten years or so, these professors and new community friends became instant mentors because they lived their values. To me, their whole existence seemed to reflect a deep engagement in the world. They had a profound impact on me, as did the entire network of people gathered to fight the Brumley Dam project. They demonstrated that loving one's neighbor is sometimes best done through political engagement rather than just showing up at someone's house to read the Bible, or going to church and placing money in the offering plate. My academic papers began to reflect these experiences as I focused on social justice for my remaining semesters.

Though required courses had taken up most of my credit hours, I had one remaining slot for an elective during my senior year. I decided to use it for Steve Fisher's course, Politics of Appalachia, a survey of the scholarship and action in the region, including the Appalachian Studies Association, which Steve had just helped organize in 1977. In the first week of class, we plunged into root causes of Appalachian poverty. Soon after, we studied how local color writers and missionaries had created stereotypes and Appalachian myths that discouraged readers from believing in people's ability to change the world around them. Early in the semester, we dismantled Jack Weller's *Yesterday's People* and its arguments about Appalachian backwardness. A West Virginian by birth, Steve showed us how the people living in the mountains have suffered from the extraction of their region's commodities like coal and timber, with few profits being sent back to pay for education or infrastructure. We learned how, even as our resources helped generate national wealth, we had fallen behind the rest of the country in income, education, and development. The disparities I had witnessed during my own mountain experiences were similar throughout all of Appalachia, especially in the coalfields where poverty was much worse than in our agricultural region. Throughout Appalachia, people had long been stereotyped for being violent, lazy, and not keeping up. They had been victimized and then blamed.

Most of the students in my class came from Appalachia. Together we studied how the coal industries first lured rural mountain refugees, immigrants, and African American sharecroppers from the Deep South into their coal camps with promises of jobs, only to entrap them in debt peonage. We read about how the coal bosses paid the miners in scrip; and how gun thugs killed miners who organized unions to fight for health care, education for their children, and better pay for the most dangerous work in the world. We studied the causes of black lung disease, and we dissected how companies took farmland for strip mining by using broad-form deeds that allowed them to extract the spoils and leave rural communities with flooding and landslides to clean up. Then we turned to how the industry mechanized and began laying off people. Whole communities were abandoned after machines replaced human jobs. I was primed to hear this, and the information sank in like no other course I'd ever taken. Finally, I had started to find answers to the questions that had caused me to rip myself away from my grandma.

Fortunately, Steve gave us more than a laundry list of social problems. He also taught us how people with few resources, like the citizens of Brumley Gap, fought for their own advancement and protection. We read about miners' strikes and how local people sat down in protest in front of strip-mining bulldozers. We listened to protest songs such as "Which Side Are You On?" by Florence Reece. We learned about the Highlander Research and Education Center where Guy and Candie Carawan and others wrote songs on a Tennessee mountaintop, and where Dr. King and others learned "We Shall Overcome." Highlander was where Rosa Parks planned her famous sit-down bus protest as well. Suddenly our Appalachia, both its plight and responses to it, were revealed to us as central to the American story.

I began to identify as an Appalachian out of pride and as a statement of protest. I wore the moniker of "hillbilly" as a political badge and began defending mountain people verbally, which I found I needed to do sometimes even among people from the region. Most important, I was meeting people who were actively working to make our world a better place, who taught me to believe that people must be the source of their own freedom and protection. I desperately wanted to join them.

With Steve's help, I began volunteering as a researcher on a landownership study whose goal was to show how outside owners had dominated the region. Assisting an ex-Catholic priest named Patrick Ronan, I copied records from the Land Books in the Register of Deeds office in Smyth County, the non-coal county whose seat is my high school town of Marion. That work became part of the overall study of eighty counties later published as the book *Who Owns Appalachia?* The study documented how a handful of wealthy landowners controlled vast swaths of the Appalachian counties, and revealed in hard numbers who controlled the land that once belonged to independent farmers and homesteaders. The numbers showed how holding large parcels of land benefited the few. We already knew mountain landownership was antidemocratic, but now we had the numbers to prove it.

I also volunteered as often as my schedule allowed with the Human Economic Appalachian Development (HEAD) Corporation based in Berea, Kentucky. With local staffers Jack and Connie

McLanahan, I traveled to Kentucky to help lay the groundwork for organizing community gardens in the coalfields. This was the first time my agricultural background helped me in a work setting. Eastern Kentucky wasn't exactly home, but working there helped me understand land loss in a broader context.

Back on campus, I worked with my fellow resident advisor Louis Jones to organize Emory & Henry's first commemoration of Dr. Martin Luther King, Jr., a weeklong observance that included a library exhibit we put up with the help of several other students, and which culminated in a commemorative day and keynote address in the campus chapel. I drew a portrait of King to display and realized even my art could help foster social change. Throughout the years I knew Louis, an African American from North Carolina, he taught me invaluable lessons about the divisions of race on campus and beyond. He had been awarded a scholarship to Emory & Henry by a white church in his hometown. In long talks together, I came to understand how hard life was for Louis as one of only a handful of Blacks on campus. E&H's first MLK Day was our effort to build a bridge.

The overarching lesson of my Emory & Henry College experience was that learning is about active engagement rather than the passive reception of information. I learned that one has to get moving outside of campus walls in order to find answers. Similarly, I also absorbed that truly being part of a community, whether a neighborhood or campus, is not a passive act; community is an active group of involved human beings in motion that forms when people work together and go where their hearts lead. By moving, they find others already walking similar paths. These fellow travelers in turn become one's tribe, kin, or church. As Myles Horton, the founder of Highlander Center, along with Brazilian educator and activist Paulo Freire, wrote, "We make the road by walking." In other words, forging community change requires moving. Note that they said "we." That simple pronoun captures the gist of what I learned about community organizing while in school.

Youth shooting basketball at sharecropper house. Photograph by Rob Amberg.

Sowing | *1979*

earing spring break of my last semester of college, I came upon an article in *Sojourners* magazine about Koinonia Farm, a Christian community in Americus, Georgia. Koinonia's founder, Clarence Jordan, had been raised as a Southern Baptist in South Georgia and attended seminary where he became a biblical scholar specializing in Greek translation. After seminary, he and a handful of like-minded people began taking the notion of biblical *koinonia* (Greek for community) literally. This came to mean moving into a village together in the late 1940s, sharing resources, raising their food on land they owned in common near where Clarence grew up, and committing themselves to radical love of all people regardless of race. In Georgia, terms like *racial reconciliation* were at that time as deadly as rattlesnakes. In taking up those serpents, the Koinonia community not only talked about reconciliation but became literal neighbors to former sharecroppers, and even started a low-income housing project on their farm. That initiative would later morph into the organization Habitat for Humanity under community member Millard Fuller's leadership. Although the community cohered internally, their so-called race-mixing soon triggered the surrounding white community to retaliate with violence and ostracize the newcomers economically.

Clarence's best-known New Testament writings, translated from the original *Koine*, retell the story of Jesus set in mid-twentieth-century rural Georgia. His biblical characters are members of a Georgia farming community where Jesus preaches about the reconciliation between rural Black and white people. His version of the familiar Good Samaritan parable, for example, depicts a Black man of modest means finding and rescuing an injured white man in a ditch, after white church leaders had passed him by on the other side of the road on their way to prayer meeting. In this vernacular style, Clarence translated Jesus's words into subtle but biting critiques against racism and organized mainstream American Christianity, where white Christians often tacitly, if not openly, supported segregation. Clarence died in 1969, a decade before I arrived at Koinonia, but as the *Sojourners* article had reported, the community he helped found still thrived. Finding emphases on both farming and social justice in the same place, I had to go. I dropped any preexisting plans for spring break and drove to Americus, which led to my volunteering there for the summer after graduation.

I chose the garden crew for my work assignment and soon became one of their most enthusiastic volunteers. The Koinonia garden was a two-acre organic plot that provided much of the food for the Koinonia Partners and volunteers. I weeded, mulched, planted, harvested, and sweated, as this was the hottest climate I'd ever experienced. But even stymied by the South Georgia heat, I always seemed to be one of the last to come out of the field. I beamed when one volunteer said, "You must be a farmer at heart." I was, of course.

Surrounding our houses, office, community center, washhouse, and garden was a 440-acre farm where community members and several full-time employees worked the production agriculture that helped pay the bills for the community. While we were at work in the vegetable garden, it was common to see drivers in large tractors with air-conditioned cabs cultivating corn, soybeans, and peanuts in Koinonia's adjacent fields. Pecan trees and grapes that grew in beautiful groves nearby were also part of the diversified operation. This was the first time I had witnessed that scale of commercial crop production up close, but it made sense how all the pieces fit together and I felt a kinship with the farmers, wishing quietly I could have been one of them.

A few organic purists on our crew were offended by both the large equipment and the farm's use of integrated pest management, which called for some pesticide spraying, and even occasional crop dusting by airplanes. But since the farm was paying our way, no one argued vehemently that we should live by our handwork alone—which, after all, paid us nothing but produce on the table. We knew firsthand what a couple of organic acres of garden felt like to work, and realized that even though we grew good healthy food and saved the community on food bills, we could not pay for the rest of our needs with manual labor. Meanwhile, Ebbie Markarios, the farm manager, had helped turn Koinonia's farm into one of the most successful in the county. The Sumter County agricultural agents even made the community's fields an example they used to teach other farmers about innovative practices, a far cry from the boycotts of earlier decades.

Unlike the farm, we managed our garden completely without resorting to pesticides or synthetic fertilizers, and by mid-June it overflowed with produce. After freezing and canning as much as the community could use, we still had a large surplus. We decided that we should try to share the produce with people who might need it. I volunteered at the end of a hot day to drive with Kathy, the garden manager, to Americus, some seven miles away to try to find a home for the extra food. After painting a colorful sign on plywood that read FRESH VEGETABLES, we loaded Koinonia's old red pickup with baskets and produce. Kathy drove us to one of the poorest African American neighborhoods in town, parking along a street lined with old gray, unpainted houses. Within minutes, people, mostly elderly, began to emerge from their houses and descend from their porches to survey our melons, beans, okra, peppers, corn, and tomatoes. From the look of the neighborhood, its streets empty of cars except junked ones, the residents had no transportation. The closest grocery store was miles away. At the time, I had not yet heard the term *food desert*, but this was certainly one. Some of the people approaching our truck said it was the first fresh produce they had seen that year.

With no profit motive for being in Americus, our prices must have seemed strange. When people asked, "How much is that?" pointing to eggplants our crew had picked only a few hours before, we were so delighted they wanted to eat it that we would have been happy to offer it for free. But we didn't want to appear patronizing either, instead searching for a happy medium between profiting and giving stuff away. "Fifty cents for a bagful," Kathy replied. As we helped bag the produce, we explained that Koinonia's garden was primarily for our own use, and that the low prices we offered were simply because we were trying to share the bounty with neighbors. "We're just trying to cover our expenses," Kathy said, exuding altruism and a little shyness at the same time. "We didn't want to throw food away when people can use it."

The poverty surrounding us was evidence of the century-long aftermath of slavery; how could we then profit from it? Conscious of our whiteness, Kathy and I knew our actions were nothing but a mix of privilege and charity, and that our food would change nothing in the long run, but we hoped that at the very least an act of kindness and respect could help chip away at the racial barriers built over centuries. And that for a night or two during the weeks we returned with more produce to sell, some elderly residents and their dependents did eat healthier food. After we stopped, we also knew that too many people would go back to eating what they could scrape together from the convenience store and maybe a little something they grew themselves outside their kitchen door. The food shortage stemmed from many factors, including underemployment and poverty, a lack of land and equipment with which to grow gardens, and the fact that the biggest grocery chains catered only to the white middle class. This left the poorest people with the least reliable transportation to make do with the detritus of our food system, or the altruism of do-gooders like us.

After they bought their produce, we watched these people who had worked all their lives—a good number of them as agricultural laborers or as sharecroppers, they told us—carry the bags back to their unpainted shotgun houses. Back on the porch, some were greeted by grandchildren who asked what was in the bags; some of those children, we imagined, might never have seen some of the vegetables before. We had many repeat customers week to week, but after our flush of produce was gone, I never went back. Still, those brief exchanges had left their mark on me. We had met people eager to eat food we raised, and we felt good about some of the verbal exchanges the food inspired, yet we drove away both sad and angry that the world was so unequal. Gestures like ours, we felt, did more to highlight the barriers between people than break them down.

As we weeded in the garden the next day, Kathy talked with the rest of the crew about our lopsided exchanges in Americus. We all agreed that the recipients had gotten something of value, and that our reward had been seeing people appreciate what we grew. But the disparity between wealth and poverty weighed on us. That we owned no land and made no money from our work in the garden for the summer was in no way comparable to the lives of the former sharecroppers we met. Our life was the opposite of sharecropping or living in substandard housing with no future prospects. We were volunteers, free to come and go, take breaks for refreshments while sitting in front of a fan. Moreover, we got a strong sense that Koinonia belonged to us, too, even after only a few weeks—so much so that I could drive into town with Kathy and act as if the produce was ours to sell. All we really needed in return was to see people appreciate what we grew. But we were not naive. We knew we had done nothing in the end to alleviate poverty, which is a main cause of food inequality.

By chance that summer I had picked up a copy of *All God's Dangers: The Life of Nate Shaw* from a shelf in our household's library. Reading the words of a Black sharecropper in South Georgia gave me new insights into the exploitation and indebtedness of the Jim Crow period, as well as how the resurgence of white supremacy following Reconstruction was still visible in the world around us in which African American people still owned almost no land and had few good prospects for work in decent jobs.

Of course, there was one major difference between rural life during Shaw's 1930s and that of the late 1970s: increased mechanization. During the nearly fifty years since the Great Depression, agribusiness had introduced machinery and pesticides, which meant that human beings were no longer needed as much in the fields for planting, weeding, and harvesting cotton and other row crops. These major shifts had put many of the rural poor, many of them descended from enslaved people, out of work entirely, often forcing them to move from sharecropper shacks into southern small-town and city slums. Some who were able to leave joined the Great Migration northward, but the old, the tired, and the poorest—like those we had met in Americus—had no escape route.

Thanks to the Koinonia housing model, some former sharecroppers had moved into their own homes nearby. This major break in the pattern of dependency gave our group of volunteers a chance to talk with these new homeowners about economics in the present as well as their former life of sharecropping. Speaking with neighbors while reading Nate Shaw's account of sharecropping helped me understand how much of a privilege it is to call a house and farm one's own. Even my ancestors, as poor as they were, had owned land, in part, because of our color.

Though my family members had possessed only small parcels in the Virginia Blue Ridge, they used those places to earn equity, and to dream the American Dream, in real, if small, ways. When they sold their farms, even if it was because farming no longer paid, most descendants gained places in the suburbs, thereby still owning a small part of America. Though family farmers were fast losing their hold on farm ownership where I was from, in South Georgia I witnessed an even worse agricultural tragedy in which sharecroppers, most of them descendants of enslaved people, had worked for generations but never gained land or economic security to begin with. They had given their lives to agriculture, but had nothing to pass on to the next generation. Worse, they often died in an unyielding debt that entrapped generations in poverty. In Sumter County and many places like it, economic disparity was obviously tied to racism.

Nate Shaw summarized the problem by showing that certain people knowingly beat the profit out of others:

> I never tried to beat nobody out of nothin since
> I been in this world, never has, but I understands

that there's a whole class of people tries to beat the
other class of people out of what they has. I've had
it put on me; I've seen it put on others, with these
eyes. O, it's plain: if every man thoroughly got his
rights, there wouldn't be so many rich people in
the world—I spied that a long time ago. . . . O,
it's desperately wrong. . : . I found out all of that
because they tried to take I don't know what all
away from me.*

Shaw's story goes on to show that the organization he joined,
the Southern Tenant Farmers' Union, made some headway against
those who beat his people out of what they had. The organization
won some landless workers some labor rights, gaining the support
of Eleanor Roosevelt and others, who, in turn, started an organization called the National Sharecroppers Fund (NSF). Through the
combined efforts of the sharecroppers and their supporters, the
Rural Resettlement Administration of the USDA responded during
the Great Depression with ownership loans to landless farmers, the
only land reform effort our nation ever championed.

However, though hundreds of Black, Native American, and white
farmers received loans through this effort, the timing was off, for
just as these new loan recipients were going into business at a small
scale, large farms had begun mechanizing, increasing their acreage,
and dominating national markets. By then, a new farmer with "forty
acres and a mule"—a phrase that originated with a promise first
made during the Civil War by General William Tecumseh Sherman
in January of 1865, shortly after his March to the Sea—had to compete against farmers controlling hundreds, even thousands, of acres
and the large equipment required to work it. A major contributor to
farm inequality was the USDA's issue of price supports to farmers

---

* Theodore Rosengarten, *All God's Dangers: The Life of Nate Shaw* (New York:
Alfred A. Knopf, 1974), 544–45.

regardless of farm size. Through the Agricultural Marketing Act of 1929, the government reduced the reserves of grain crops and gave farmers a floor price that supported their major crops regardless of the quantity grown. This was followed by the Agricultural Adjustment Act, created during the New Deal by the USDA in 1933, which paid farmers to take fields out of production, resulting in sharecroppers being thrown off the land. The great irony here is that just as the Rural Resettlement Administration came into being in 1935 to help landless people buy farms, the USDA was already facilitating large farm consolidation. As the government gave landless farmers a start on a small piece of land, giving the appearance of equalizing the playing field, the game had in fact already been won by large-scale farms before these new players ever left the bench.

Working in Koinonia's garden for a summer showed me that there had never been any "good old days" for most southern farmworkers. When I met sharecroppers and their descendants in the surrounding communities, it was easy to understand how their lives connected to the in-town poverty I witnessed. Though once I believed that love and generosity could break down barriers between people, my Koinonia experience showed me that addressing racial discrimination, just like changing an agricultural system rooted in social inequality, required both organizing and legal challenges.

Also, as I chopped in the soil and spread straw by hand alongside my friends on the garden crew, I realized that not even our labor for good had anything to do with solving the larger inequalities of agriculture. At least we were eating what we raised, we said, and as far as I knew, we weren't making the problems of inequality and the misuse of land and people any worse. But by summer's end every one of us knew that gardening organically would not bring justice to the descendants of sharecroppers.

Fortunately, gardening was only part of the story of Koinonia. Standing on that Georgia land owned by a Christian community dedicated to reconciliation, I was constantly reminded that residents had risked their lives for change. In the 1940s, when sharecropping was at its height, African Americans and whites had risked owning property together. In reaction, the white supremacists ostracized members' children from local schools. Local businesses refused to sell any goods to the farm residents. And Klan members fire-bombed and machine-gunned their homes. Miraculously, no one was killed, but the Partners spent many nights huddled on their floors dodging bullets.

Koinonia's survival strategy in the midst of the boycott had been to construct a commercial kitchen from which members and neighbors made and sold products like candied pecans and peanuts from their farm and shipped them by US mail around the nation. Since it is a federal offense to tamper with the mail, this strategy helped circumvent the boycott. Catholic activist Dorothy Day and other national figures lent their names to the cause. After the Koinonia community secured their survival through mail order, they started building houses and selling them at no interest to poor people so they could have a start at owning a little piece of land and a decent house. Such acts were simple and seemingly benign on the surface, but were profoundly political in their context. As with Jesus advocating for reconciliation in a deeply divided society, such acts of justice can get you killed.

Though the overt attacks at Koinonia had ended by the time I arrived, the war against African Americans was still on. Police brutality continued. Black farmers still owned almost no land at all in our section of the county. The only signs of African American land possession were their churches. I could only guess at how many hours of sharecropper labor it took to build those strongholds of community. Before arriving, I had known something about inequality and I had studied dispossession in the coalfields of Appalachia; but that summer I had witnessed apartheid, and I had started to understand the stakes involved in breaking it down.

As a result, I began to question whether lifestyles were enough to effect change. I knew that the Partners had adopted what some referred to as "downward mobility." Their commitment was to give up personal possessions, live on five dollars a week, use community cars only when necessary, and walk or ride bikes otherwise. We ate vegetarian food raised on the farm, and bought clothes from the Red Mushroom, a secondhand store run by Koinonia. Most would have said we were doing all of this to fight inequality. "Live simply so others can simply live," was a popular slogan then.

In contrast, our African American neighbors in the villages and those working at Koinonia were only in the beginning stages of owning anything. Few had any advantages of higher education or inheritance from family. Buying a house with no interest through Koinonia was their first hint of owning any part of the American Dream. Most were struggling to climb one rung upward if they were moving at all.

Troubled by this disparity, I began to acknowledge that people who have privilege should address it head-on and take steps to dismantle the barriers that make it possible, but I also understood that the oppressed must rise up to overcome their setbacks. The question was how the two groups heading in opposite directions could find common ground. One answer that we came up with was, for starters, those who have power must be quiet and listen to those who do not have it. Fortunately, living at Koinonia provided opportunities for this kind of exchange. One of the best examples for me was our garden crew's visit with Mr. Bo Johnson, a former sharecropper and, by then, a longtime farmer at Koinonia. He was the first, along with his wife Emma, to purchase a house in one of Koinonia's villages.

Sitting with him and listening to his story of growing up in South Georgia was like hearing the Georgia clay itself talk. He told us how he had struggled to gain the stability he now had at Koinonia, where he now made a decent salary and enjoyed some autonomy and pride in his work. Johnson was one of the farmers I watched regularly driving through fields on combines or in the enclosed cabs of tractors as I worked in the garden. I thought many times about the expertise he had accumulated, starting back when he was doing handwork or walking behind mules, all for the white boss. So much of his and others' labor had helped whites own more of the country. His sweat had contributed to their equity and not his, favoring the descendants of plantation owners for generations to come. Though the inequality was still palpable in the red soil on which we sat and listened, Mr. Johnson taught us about reconciliation and love by choosing not to treat our mostly white group as part of the problem, but as potential allies in the fight for equality. His gift to us in the midst of so much racism was to inspire us to believe we youths could be part of the ongoing movement for justice.

Coal train, eastern West Virginia, 1993. Photograph by Rob Amberg.

Digging | *1979–80*

*D*uring my summer at Koinonia, I received a job offer to return to work in Appalachian Virginia and Kentucky with the nonprofit HEAD Corporation, one of the organizations I'd volunteered with while in college. The full-time job was to help organize rural community gardens in the coalfields. I knew that taking the job would mean leaving Koinonia's community for a more isolated place. But my pull to work in my own region, particularly to help people in coal camps raise their own food, was strong. Earning a salary was also a draw. I took the job.

As I drove westward from the Valley of Virginia across the Alleghenies in late September, I noticed the land and the culture defined by coal seams and its extraction were not at all like the farms of the Valley of Virginia and its Blue Ridge I knew so well. The terrain in eastern Kentucky was much steeper and the hollows darker than in Marion or Franklin County. Hardest to witness were the parts of the mountains where men had gouged the hills apart to get at the money inside. I felt as if I was driving into a war zone rather than revisiting the nurturing mountains I had grown up in. In some places, whole peaks had been blown off with dynamite, and strip-mine benches were carved out of the mountainsides by huge earthmoving equipment now looming above the road. Machinery bigger than I'd ever seen had scooped out the yellow shale, causing silt to wash into the streams below. Reclamation amounted to planting cover crops like lespedeza on the stripped hills, but there was little sign of trees ever coming back.

As I drove through the old coal camps, many named after coal companies like Vicco and Clinchco, I passed cottages tightly sandwiched between the road and muddy creeks. I met countless coal trucks barreling by on narrow, dusty roads within feet of run-down, discolored homes. It was clear that while coal still held sway economically, the old coal camps where miners had once worked in the deep shafts were now filled with mostly unemployed people. Their ancestors had moved into the towns to work at the turn of the twentieth century, back when deep mines recruited hand diggers. Now, even though machines continued to churn out the bituminous coal, and companies were still moving it out of the region by the trainload daily, the good jobs had dwindled and poverty grew worse. In 1979, some mines already looked abandoned, and it was clear the coal jobs were not coming back. Knowing this, many able-bodied workers had left for manufacturing jobs in the North and Southeast, but as I had witnessed before in similar contexts, the oldest and disabled were left behind in old homes, and were forced to fend for themselves. Black lung disease and job-related injuries had also left many sick and unable to work or move out. These people would be my constituency; I would try to help them grow food.

My very first week on the job, I hit the road with the goal of surveying organizations already at work on food issues: from the Maryknoll sisters working in a soup kitchen in Big Stone Gap, Virginia, to Community Action employees giving out food stamps and nutrition information in Breathitt County, Kentucky. I sought out any community advocate I could find with any interest in food and agriculture. My search was for signs of hope and a fighting spirit that might be poking up like sprigs of green through an old strip mine. Upon finding any such sign, I would try to assist the people already at work and help spread their influence to other communi-ties. Newly arrived from Koinonia, my batteries were charged, my optimism was high, and I plunged into the work.

My first and most important contact for community gardening was Nancy Coles, a stout woman in her late sixties living in an old community seemingly devoid of any businesses. I met her first at a Community Action meeting in Hazard. She told me her coal miner husband had died in a mining fire. Now a widow, Nancy, after raising her children on a limited income, had helped neighbors living in the old mining town organize the Concerned Citizens of Barfield, and had written and received a small grant to build a greenhouse. Under her leadership, the community built a plastic-covered Quonset-style structure fifty feet from her back door on a small piece of flat land beside the main dirt road winding through her neighborhood. As with other former coal camps I'd passed through, Barfield was a community of mostly landless people, many of them disabled and unemployed. Nancy returned to memories of her family's connections to agriculture, and applied what she knew to the little piece of land in back of her house.

For Nancy and her neighbors, government assistance was never enough to survive on. They needed supplemental income. They needed better nutrition. The nearest grocery store, whose produce section offered only bananas, onions, and potatoes, was some twenty curvy—and, in winter, icy—miles away. Some Barfield residents had no cars. Public transportation was nonexistent. These were white people with few resources—a whole community of them trying to figure out to survive through their economic anxieties. And this was just one among many towns like it in Central Appalachia.

Soon after my arrival in Hindman, Kentucky, where I lived, Nancy invited me to drive to her community to see the greenhouse for myself. When I got to Barfield the next week, she greeted me at the front of her old house and walked me to the kitchen. We sat and drank a cup of coffee together first, then we went out her back door and entered the plastic-covered greenhouse, the newest and cheeriest structure anywhere around. It measured some thirty by sixty feet. Even in the fall, Nancy and her neighbors had plants growing inside. A vegetable garden filled with cold-hardy plants flourished nearby. This was some of the best nutritious food around, she said. A picture of the Barfield community's green plants growing amid scarcity would never have made it onto the cover of *Organic Gardening* magazine, but it did show how the human spirit can replenish itself, even in the most trying circumstances.

I visited with Nancy at least three times before she told me the rest of the story of the community greenhouse. "You have to take what I'm going to tell you knowing I'm here to help people," Nancy said, lowering her voice. I nodded, indicating that I would do nothing to hurt her cause. She continued, "What we do here is we raise as much of our own food as possible. Then those savings on our food bill let us take our food stamps and sell them to others who can use them. Then we use the food stamp money for medical supplies and other things we have to buy with cash."

I'd heard all the critiques about people living on welfare and not wanting to work and so on, some of them from people I knew well. But here were people on assistance trying hard to be productive in an economic desert. After their jobs went away, and with nowhere else to turn, they had invented means to help themselves by reorganizing their scant resources for maximum benefit. In reality, instead of defrauding the government, they were doubling their food stamps' effectiveness. Growing produce, of course, is no crime. Plus, as my job description directed me to enact with HEAD, Nancy was a perfect example of someone helping people take their food production into their own hands, even if in an unlikely way. Perhaps selling food stamps was illegal on paper, but I knew this was a moral act of food self-sufficiency, part of a general aim that even USDA officials would applaud, that is, if they were kept in the dark about the particulars.

During my regular drives to Nancy's community over the coming year, trying to learn and help share their story with others by writing and printing a brochure about Barfield, I started to realize that using romantic language about its residents being attached to particular places, much like the farmers I grew up with, was just wrong. Though some residents said their parents were buried nearby and that it would be hard to leave them, for most, staying in Barfield was more about making do and necessity than attachment to tradition. The real story was that coal companies had lured people away from agriculture, used them up, and then left them behind with no land. What I saw was coal's aftershock. But to flee such a predicament, you have to have some money, decent health, strength, access to transportation, gas, and a place to go. A new start elsewhere requires knowledge and a network. Pulling up what few roots one has is only the beginning. Too many who leave without having connections in another place end up living in cars on some city backstreet.

Before arriving in Kentucky, I had learned from Steve Fisher at Emory & Henry how coal companies bought up much of the coal as early as the nineteenth century, contriving to take advantage of farmers who didn't know what lay under their soil. I had learned how immigrants and exiles from other industries had gone there to seek jobs by the thousands. Now, by moving into the middle of what was left of the economy in 1979, I was witness to what happens when the sole economic driver of a place leaves people behind. Though coal was headed eastward every day toward Norfolk's ports and eventually to coal-burning power plants all around the world, there were no new schools, roads, bridges, or even hospitals being built as repayment. People living not half a mile from some of the nation's richest coal seams were suffering from poverty and a lack of resources that were as bad as it gets in America.

If my agricultural romanticism was still breathing after seeing my own family's farms come under fire, followed by witnessing how race and sharecropping had created a caste system in the Deep South, then my work in the heart of Central Appalachia was its coup de grâce. Nonetheless, I was heartened to see that people living with so little still had the will to grow vegetables. I drew much solace from the Barfield example and a few others like it. Using their stories, our organization helped raise money to start other groups. To acquire a greenhouse, communities first had to form an organization, elect leaders, and draw up work plans. I had no delusions that this community gardening model was going to reverse the effects of absentee ownership and extractive economics, but it was a way for people to have better nutrition and a little spending money right away. To struggle for justice, one has to eat. In a newsletter, I wrote: "Nancy and the people of Barfield never asked for a handout. They simply made a way to feed themselves." They had demonstrated that food security can be achieved only when the production of food is controlled by the people themselves.

Though I tried hard to remain positive by championing movers and shakers like Nancy, the coalfields began to take their toll on my morale after about six months. Driving alone on the slurried roads and jockeying for position among coal trucks, I started to realize how badly I missed seeing open farmland. I was homesick for family. In an attempt to create a sense of home, I planted a garden on an open slope of land alongside the old store building where I lived. My little plot of Black-Seeded Simpson lettuce looked minuscule on the steep hillside overshadowed by the yellow shale road cut, but it was my one small attempt at agricultural optimism in the otherwise depressing scene outside my window. I also dug out a flat space under the old store where I built a chicken coop, then bought six pullets to raise. Later as I brought my first eggs and a handful of lettuce leaves into the kitchen in early March to share with my housemates, I realized I was practicing some of what I preached. But I also realized how much growing food must be a communal and familial act. I was gardening and raising chickens alone. Though a scattered group of like-minded people lived in the county, our gatherings were sporadic. Many of us worked hard to bring about change, but too few of us were nurturing ourselves and one another. When we did find time to get together, we too often resorted to drinking and forgetting, rather than focusing on rejuvenation. The boost I had taken from Koinonia's discussions about hope and change was wearing thin.

Revealing how homesick I was, when I passed a random farmer still hanging on to land along some back road I nearly always pulled off to talk with him or her about cows or an apple tree, a field of sweet corn or a hive of honeybees. Like an expatriate, my attraction to home places had intensified with distance, and my radar was up for any signs of the old country. Back home, Grandma's health had worsened, but Grandpa, though growing older, was still at home working his land with my parents' help. The old cabin was still back in Woolwine, but getting there now took nearly a day's drive. That's how bad the coalfield roads were. When I returned to park in front of my apartment in the old store building at night, my car was often covered in coal slurry, and my soul also bore the dust and scars of what I had seen and driven through. At my lowest ebb, a Mennonite friend in a neighboring county introduced me to the writings of Wendell Berry. "You'll eat up what he has to say," he said, pun intended.

That year, Kentucky's native son provided me with poetic words that described why farming had been such a central inspiration for my life and why its absence had brought about my malaise. I read Berry's groundbreaking book *The Unsettling of America: Culture and Agriculture*, which had just been released. After devouring that, I started on his novels and poetry. As most who have read him know, Berry's spiritual and agrarian language reaches us in places we didn't know we had inside us. By 1979, he had become a spokesman for throngs of Americans who lamented the loss of rural communities and were trying to revive small farming, and now I was joining them as a devotee. He was a rural visionary, possessing an authenticity that comes from being rooted in place and tradition. Berry himself was a farmer who lived among other farmers and his writing showed it. For me, he put into words so many of my joys and lamentations associated with home and its absence.

In January of 1980, I got word about a spring small farm conference at the University of Kentucky where Berry would be speaking. Making the excuse to my boss that this gathering would be directly relevant to my work in the coalfields, I went to the gathering in Lexington, and especially to hear Berry. After driving out of the mountains and toward the rolling bluegrass section of the state, I was heartened to walk into the large conference center and see hundreds of people gathered to launch Kentucky's burgeoning alternative farm movement. Every direction I looked, there were young people—all of them white—trying hard to look like alternative farmers, their boots and overalls conveying an identity combining a new emphasis on sustainability with an appreciation of the agrarian values of old. Shortly after I registered at the front table, I saw the crowds gathering in the hallway outside one meeting room and I knew who was holding forth inside. I squeezed as close to the doorway as possible to hear Wendell's every word.

He didn't speak about agricultural politics or of America's unsettling that day, however. Instead, his topic was draft horses. Like spiritual seekers, those of us crowding inside and around the doorway were eager to hear whatever he had to say about pretty much anything. Draft horse management wasn't exactly the sermon I needed—I had wanted to hear something to convince me our country still had a soul; a new farm language to revive me from my coalfield depression; some good old agricultural religion, a farm redemption—but at least I got to see the man himself.

The heroes in Berry's literature are typically members of a community of farmers—with the Amish being a prime example—who have remained in place for generations, the ones who intentionally put roots down, saying, "This is the place" and possess "the tendency to stay put," rather than live transiently, as he wrote in *The Unsettling of America.* He laments the loss of the agrarian ideal embraced by Thomas Jefferson and other founders that has been usurped by an unbridled corporate agriculture, which in turn has consolidated both production and distribution into ever greater holdings. As farms have grown ever larger, usually with the government's aid and blessing, the new family-sized operations lose out. Berry helped me put into words what we are still fighting for.

Regardless of what he said about draft horses that day, both the overall meaning of the conference and simply being there made me feel as if I had been to a tent revival meeting. My spirit felt renewed. Yet as I drove back the next day into the steep, ever-tightening hollows of the coalfields, passing by dirty creeks and ramshackle houses in company towns, the words about new farming that I'd heard at the farm conference—seemingly on another lighter and more beautiful planet—began to sound like distant echoes. In those scarred mountains with the shanties beneath them, Wendell Berry's words about farms seemed irrelevant. The problem many living in Central Appalachia experienced was that they had no ancestors who stopped to say, "This is the place" and then declared, as true owners of property, that this is where they would remain. Their desolate coal town houses were never of their own choosing. No one who has ever lived in them felt they had arrived home there. Exploitation is at the heart of their stories, nothing like the American myth of land and freedom Jefferson and the early agrarians had championed.

As far as workers in America go, the enslaved whose children became landless sharecroppers have borne the deepest scars. But the waves of immigrant laborers from Italy and Ireland, who along with some African Americans from the plantation South flowed into the Virginias or eastern Kentucky and went straight to work digging coal and living in crowded camps, never had it much better. All over the South, the millions of African Americans who fought to possess even their own person never owned land they could call their own. Indentured servants and other immigrant workers may have built wealth for others, but rarely for themselves. One cannot be unsettled until first settling, and settling presumes the right to be somewhere. The coal towns were never such places, any more than the plantations of Georgia were.

These were the kinds of thoughts filling my mind as I pulled up to the old store building near my little raised bed of lettuce. As I sat in the car a few minutes, it hit me that while I was still high on Wendell Berry, I had brought back little to share with the Nancy Coles of Appalachia, even those living within the same state. Such eloquence about alternative farming in Kentucky would have had even less to say to people of color of Georgia. Though I had only traveled a few states away from Virginia by that time, I was starting to realize that the story of America's landowning past is only relevant to a certain portion of its citizenry.

Jefferson believed landowners possess a will to fight to protect their territory. They are defenders of democracy, because if any despot or power broker attempts to unsettle them, landowners will join together. Sitting on a coalfield roadside, I knew that reality was never universally possessed. Only a few people living around me shared that kind of presumption of home. In fact, some Americans nearby did not have enough good food to eat that night. From where could their strength to protect or change this country come?

My thoughts turned to my Endicott ancestors in Franklin County. Though poor and steep, their land had stuck under their fingernails, and it provided them at least a tenuous hold on freedom. Even if they had arrived in the Blue Ridge with only an axe, a mule, and a liquor still they brought over the Wagon Road on Conestoga wagons, they had at least found and claimed, or squatted on, a few acres and staked a claim. By the "sweat of their brow" they had gained a spirit of farm ownership and passed it down. From them I had inherited the seeds of both my faith in agriculture and my fighting spirit.

Such a feeling for land and freedom among the yeomanry was the crux of Jefferson's agrarian ideal. He believed, as he said in his *Notes on Virginia*, that small farmers are the "chosen people of God," and the very backbone of American democracy. I had to admit that agrarianism had validity—at least for some. I have to believe that though some of my ancestor farmers were as poor as the dirt they worked, their ownership of farms did lead eventually to my driving to Lexington and my standing alongside others at the University of Kentucky knowing that Mr. Berry's every word was for me.

Yet, as I walked into the old store building to my bedroom, some critical questions arose regarding the two worlds I had inhabited in a single day. Foremost among them, I began to wonder how white landowners that Berry said were being unsettled in the twentieth century would see themselves in the greater arc of American history if they became landless. Which camp would they join after their unsettling? Would these newly displaced farmers, and other rural workers like them—many of them becoming landless for the first time in their family's history—identify with the greater number of landless people who never owned any American ground to begin with? Or would they more readily identify with the remaining white landowners who had gained an advantage from their losses? In other words, would the newly unsettled whites identify with the "haves" or the "have-nots"? As an organizer, I sensed the answers to those questions could dominate our political and personal debates in this country, including our debates about agriculture, for years to come.

Of course, we know now how many of those rural people have characterized their own losses. Many have turned to blame rather than solidarity with the others who have been left out of the American Dream. The major difference between "used-to-haves" and "have-nots" has come to mean that the people in the former category are incensed that something once theirs is now gone. They believed that if they continued working hard, they would always be among those in control of this country, just as Jefferson had said about landowners. In contrast, the working poor never felt anything like that kind of prerogative. The reality is that Jefferson's agrarianism ignored the fact there have always been two Americas, the first being the enslaved people and the indentured workers who worked to enrich an agricultural elite, and the second made up of landowners with the privilege of ownership. Their will to fight for their freedom would have to come from two very different sources. Jefferson's rhetoric was an attempt to define democracy without doing the hard work of reconciling the two sides of agriculture. He died still owning slaves, leaving us with a divide between the owners and the owned that is still with us today. To speak about agricultural justice, we cannot just pick up the debate today with the unsettling of those who once had farmland. We have to start by asking what it is about our agriculture that prevented hardworking farm people from ever owning land to begin with. From this query would come a different source of democratic values based on equal access to land.

Thinking through all this made me wonder where my sympathy for the landless had come from. Had I inherited it from my people who had worked as indentured servants? Or before that, from the landless seekers in Scotland or Ireland? Was it a reflection of the humility in my grandfather's words about the "little man"? Had the justice-oriented parables from the Bible I had grown up with come alive through my experiences? Had the poor, the landless, and the wanderer taken on real names of people I knew? As I got into bed that night, I retraced in my mind the path that had taken me to this desolate roadside in

Central Appalachia. Why had I had set aside my personal dream of farming to work for social justice? Then, larger questions surfaced: namely, how had the new agrarian movement divorced itself from the social justice tradition, leaving the cause of the poor and the landless out of the discussion of alternative agriculture altogether, making these two places I had been in on the same day seem like two completely different universes when in fact they were in the same state?

There were very few people like me who were living in both worlds I had traveled in during the same weekend. For a day and night I had eagerly joined the mobile and expectant ones in Lexington. By and large, we were middle-class people—you could tell by the brands of our work clothes and boots—dreaming of being farm owners again. We collectively believed that corporations had done our farmers wrong, and we believed we could make things right again. We wanted to set the course back toward community-based agriculture. We were set on starting a new farm movement, and we were advancing with all the confidence of people who owned America.

But during both the weeks leading up to Lexington and after, I was living among people who were part of a different genesis of agriculture. The people of Barfield and other communities like it started greenhouses for their own sustenance, in an unglamorous land of strip mines, food stamps, and disability checks. If one of their leaders, like Nancy Coles, an older, working-poor woman, had limped into Lexington wearing faded polyester clothes, she probably would have felt out of place in the new farm movement gathering at the university. Would participants have recognized the strong resonance between the two different geneses? Would they have noticed the spark of caring that had ignited Nancy's desire to start growing something local, which had spread through her community and influenced other communities in the same way the alternative farmers wished to do? I believe so, if they had only had the opportunity to listen to her. Wasn't her hope in agriculture kindled by the same flame of liberty that had given America its drive for democracy over two hundred years before? I doubt Jefferson would have said that

Nancy's people are of the same ilk as the yeomanry he championed, but I decided that night that I would say to Jefferson or any agrarian today that anyone with Nancy's will to grow food on a little piece of land—regardless of age, color, income, or history of ownership—is an essential vertebra in the backbone of our democracy. Though they may come from a different origin, their belief in a new America is just as crucial as anyone's.

Jim Smyre and family planting tobacco, 1987. Photograph by Rob Amberg.

Cultivating | *1980–81*

*T*he springtime sky seemed to expand as I left Kentucky and passed through the Valley of Virginia for an interview at the Graham Center, the Rural Advancement Fund's organic demonstration farm situated in North Carolina's Anson County, on the South Carolina border. Upon seeing the ad for garden manager in a newsletter I received that spring, I knew immediately that I wanted the job. I had to admit that I was desperate to leave the coalfields. Living on the north side of a roadcut, where the sun rose as late as eleven, and jockeying with coal trucks every day had taken its toll. Also, a personal relationship was going sour, and I was sure the place we lived had as much to do with the failure as any personality clash. When I got word about the interview, I was elated that I might work on a farm again, even though the program I was applying for with VISTA (Volunteers in Service to America) paid only a subsistence wage. The whole prospect gave me a glimmer of optimism despite the loss of salary.

After an eight-hour drive, I finally reached Wadesboro, the Anson county seat, and headed southward on 742, a two-lane road leading toward the small hamlet known as Cason Old Field at the South Carolina line. After eight or so miles, I stopped at a small country store to ask directions, thinking I must have gone too far. Inside were two white men sitting in chairs in the center of the store near the Nabs rack, and another man, the store owner, leaning on the front counter. All three watched me warily. I was familiar with the "you-ain't-from-around-here" look, but this one was more hostile. Acting as if I hadn't noticed the glares, I nodded to the men in the chairs and then greeted the man at the cash register as I paid for some Lance peanuts and a drink. Then, feeling as if my purchase gave me the right, I asked how I might find a place called the Graham Center. I thought these rural men might have welcomed a place that helped farmers. Immediately, the seated ones clammed up and gave a sidelong glance as the owner sneered and almost spit. Showing off, he laid into me with these words:

"Boy, you better turn around right now and go back to where you come from. There ain't nothing down there but niggers and white women having sex. They ain't no real farm down there, just Yankees pretending to farm with government money." More explicit and vile language followed. I quickly took my change and walked out, wishing I'd never stopped. But in the midst of his tirade, the store owner had said the words, "down there," so I took that as an unintended hint and continued southward. I found the Center not three miles farther down the same road, almost within sight of South Carolina. I should have trusted the odometer.

I mentioned the encounter to my potential supervisor, Mark Epp, as soon as I arrived at the Graham Center office, who responded, "Oh, you ran into Mr. Norwood, the Dragon of the local KKK." I replied that the farm must be doing something right to garner the wrath of such a man. And I thought to myself, where else could I have found like-minded people advocating for organic farming for African American and other limited-resource farmers; for both social justice *and* sustainable farming practices in the same place? I learned while at the Center that alongside agricultural advocacy, racial justice advocacy had always been part of its history.

The Rural Advancement Fund's parent organization, the National Sharecroppers Fund, which originated in the 1930s and was still in existence as a related lobbying institution, had been formed to provide financial and lobbying support for the integrated Southern Tenant Farmers' Union, the same organization Nate Shaw of *All God's Dangers* had joined. Leaders such as First Lady Eleanor Roosevelt, North Carolina senator Frank Porter Graham (for whom the Center was named), A. Philip Randolph, and Fay Bennett Watts were among its luminaries. For decades, the NSF advocated for landless sharecroppers at the national level and for the Rural Resettlement Administration of the USDA. And under the direction of labor leader Jim Pierce, the Rural Advancement Fund had started the Graham Center as a nonprofit training farm with the belief that organic farming was the answer for marginalized farmers. Indeed, it was the only effort I had heard of that combined sustainability with advocacy for Black and Native American farmers in the South.

The Rural Advancement Fund (RAF) began garnering grants to start the Graham Center forty years after the NSF's founding, in the midst of a poor community and on probably the worst sandy soil in North Carolina. Their reasoning was that if organic methods could work on that old worn-out cotton farm—even one with decaying sharecropper shacks—they could work anywhere. The creators thought it could be powerfully symbolic to transform an old plantation into a working organic farm. During my visit, I toured the facilities and met at least ten other people working there. Two of them had recently left Rodale, the organization that published *Organic Gardening* magazine. Meeting them, along with other Black and white staff members working together in some semblance of community, was an inspiration to me. I had just come from the coalfields where I fought for justice, but I often worked alone there. Most RAF staffers worked in the fields and in farmer outreach, but I also met some staff members who worked in the office on agricultural policy. One of them was Hope Shand, a fellow VISTA volunteer who had just recently arrived from her work in Washington, DC, and the woman who would one day be my wife. Soon after I returned to Kentucky following my visit, I received an offer letter, and I called back to take the job.

My VISTA position, which began in the fall of 1980, lasted twelve months. During my time at the Graham Center, I continued learning firsthand about race, farming, and food politics in the Deep South. I rose early every day to work as the sole caretaker in the two-acre demonstration garden situated around the main office building. I worked constantly to improve the soil where, for the first time, I could grow food for three full seasons, but also where heat, voracious pests, and the bane of the garden, Bermuda grass, tried to stymie my every move.

Prior to my arrival, the Center received a federal grant to train local farmers to do outreach and training for their neighbors. These farmer-educators were a group comprised of Black and white women and men from the surrounding counties. As part of the education team, my job was to help introduce new ideas about organic gardening, along with lessons that included everything from composting to selling at farmers markets. Feeling I had little to teach working farm people, I mostly asked them questions and got quite an education, not only about the challenges they faced individually, but also about the agricultural decline in the South in general.

Despite our minor successes, the most important lesson we learned collectively that year at the Center was that by focusing mainly on organic production, we had failed to address the root causes of the farm emergency surrounding us. It became clear that even the poorest farmers with little formal education already knew more about surviving on their land than any outsiders could teach them. The existence of any Black farmers who still owned farmland after experiencing decades of racism, low prices, and scarce government help, was proof of the power of their perseverance and astuteness. Especially in the midst of the kind of hatred in the rural South I had witnessed only a hint of at Norwood's store, we concluded that our organization's resources would be better spent on fighting the root causes of farm loss than on composting and alternative crops. Plus, we were in the midst of the first year of the Reagan administration when we could already see that big business was about to receive a boost of tax cuts, and that big farmers would also receive more benefits and even fewer pesticide restrictions. At the same time, we watched as racism subtly crept back to the front of the national political stage. We feared that any small farmers, regardless of race or gender, were about to experience a new crisis—and time has proven we were right.

The problem in farm communities, as our farmer constituents taught us, was not a lack of production knowledge, but rather a lack of rural justice. Farmers told us they had received neither fair loans nor sustainable returns with which to pay them back. We learned that access to good farmland was shrinking, especially for African American farmers. Black farmers told us how, if they received credit at all, most got smaller operating loans, often supervised by whites, and on worse terms than those received by their white counterparts. But we also learned that the treatment of the poorest white farmers was only marginally better. White landowners who operated the largest farms—the power brokers of the county—had ways of making sure they stayed in control. In reality, people like Mr. Norwood weren't the power brokers, but rather working-class henchmen, foot soldiers, and mouthpieces whose job was to foment anger among their lower-class white neighbors. There was no way that our teaching organic farming methods alone was going to dismantle those kinds of structural evils.

We also concluded that farmers should be allowed to drive their own research using public money, and that the land-grant universities' research should be directed away from food corporations and mega-farms and should work for the masses. In his groundbreaking 1973 book *Hard Tomatoes, Hard Times*, Jim Hightower was the first to show in explicit terms how land-grant universities geared their taxpayer-funded research agendas to help agribusiness. Using such research, we understood that our scant resources should be put toward organizing farmers. Our job would be to help them unite to advocate for a fair credit system and also for government research geared toward the family-sized farm. They needed family-farm-oriented laws, and their only hope was to learn how to advocate for their own needs. In short, they needed more help on how to raise hell than how to raise tomatoes.

Farmer Edna Harris, pictured with her husband, Lonnie, taking a hotline call from a distressed farmer neighbor in 1987. Photograph by Rob Amberg.

Grafting | *1982*

*A*s my VISTA year at the Graham Center was concluding, I planned to head back to see my parents and grandparents at their farm, and to explore what else might come my way. As part of my exploration, I decided a few days before departing to call up the agricultural economics and education departments at North Carolina Agricultural & Technical State University—the state's historically Black agricultural school, which is located in Greensboro—to request a visit on my way through town. Even on short notice, I found people willing to meet and talk with me. I drove northward toward Virginia, pulled into Greensboro for my scheduled appointments, and found a parking spot. As I began walking through the campus, I noticed instantly that I was the only white person in sight. I had never experienced being a minority until that moment. From the beginning, I knew the place would have a lot to teach me, if I could only listen.

I knew precious little about A&T before arriving for my visit, though I had done some general reading about historically African American land-grant universities. I did know it was an "1890 school," referring to the year of the second Morrill Act, which gave them federal support allocated by Congress. In 1862, the first Morrill Act provided land grants to eligible states (excluding the Confederate states, though they would be included after the Civil War) to pay for the construction of new agricultural institutions. These traditionally white land-grant universities came into existence at precisely the time of the Homestead Act, which provided for the settlement of the Midwest. In 1890, the second Morrill Act required former Confederate states to either demonstrate that their admissions criteria did not discriminate on the basis of race, or else designate separate institutions for people of color. Hence, the 1890 schools, coming almost three decades later during the Jim Crow period, were called "separate but equal," even though they never received equal funding or recognition.

When the landmark Supreme Court case *Brown v. Board of Education* proved that racially segregated education was both unequal and unconstitutional in 1954, the federal government mandated states with two separate agricultural research systems to combine them into one. After integration, southern states justified having two land-grant schools by emphasizing farm size rather than skin color. As a result, NC Agricultural & Technical State University (NC A&T), which remained mostly an African American school, was given charge of small farm research in North Carolina, while NC State University in Raleigh was to address the needs of commercial farmers. It sounded good on paper, but it was immediately clear on my walk through the campus how unequal the funding was, even in 1982, 120 years after the passage of the first Morrill Act. The landscaping was sparse and the buildings utilitarian, and there was little of grandeur to inspire the matriculating students.

My first meeting with some professors took place inside the ag building known as Dudley Hall, a plain rectangular brick building with unadorned institutional windows. My introductions went quite well as I explained my work in Kentucky and at the Graham Center. Hearing of my experience with the demonstration farm, one professor mentioned the A&T research farm two miles from the campus. The departmental chair then ran through the range of paid research opportunities. He also mentioned they were training high school agriculture teachers as well as technicians for the Agricultural Extension Service. Since my days as a horticulture student with Mr. Waddle, teaching agriculture had been on my radar, but I had not known there were two systems of training teachers until then. One professor admitted, "We have to do a lot with a little. The entire budget for A&T's agricultural research is only two percent of NC

State's allocation." Inequality, as was made clear that day, starts with federal allocations, which hide racialized decisions in line-item budgets. This was a silent form of discrimination, but its result was even more effective than someone spewing epithets at a country store. Yet, A&T's status as having less funding actually intrigued me, as being on the side of the underdog had become my modus operandi.

Then the departmental chair surprised me: "We have grants to offer white students," explaining that though A&T had been short-changed in general, they had money to help integrate their student body. "Because you are white, you would be a minority at our school. So, you're eligible for full tuition through a federal program called the Minority Presence Grant." Earlier in the same hour, an animal science specialist had also told me he needed a student to help manage his small sheep and hog experiment out at the research farm, saying, "With your experience on farms, I think you'd be great addition to our staff." He promised that if I came back to study, he could probably offer me a job.

As we said our good-byes, the agricultural education chair recommended that I stop by the university's agricultural extension headquarters before leaving campus to talk with them. Popping into their office on the edge of campus, I met Mr. Emery who managed a statewide initiative addressing Black land loss. He handed me a brochure, which listed a variety of financial challenges that Black farmers experience. Quickly running through the list, he specifically mentioned the problem of heirs' property when farm-owning African Americans die without wills. When I asked him to explain, Mr. Emery revealed that African American farm families started leaving agriculture due to the combined pressure of race and economics in the post–World War II era. In turn, this led to the Great Migration of rural Blacks to northern cities. Following that younger generation's departure from farms, and since then, when older farm family members who were left behind die, many are intestate (without wills). In cases where a deceased landowner is intestate, all of their heirs, no matter where they live or how little they're interested in returning to the land, must agree to keep the land in the family in order to prevent a sale. In some cases, the family can't even find all the heirs, let alone get them to agree. So in order to divide up the inheritances, that particular Black-owned land, already a dwindling resource all over the South, must be sold and the proceeds divided among surviving members of the family. "When our people's land is sold," Mr. Emery continued, "usually a white farmer or developer buys it, and it is lost forever to our community." With Black farmers already an "endangered species," this ownership predicament makes their future prospects in farming even more dire. I left Mr. Emery's office captivated by how a form of state education could combine agriculture with justice work, and how government funding could be used to address systemic social problems.

Though I had left the Graham Center that morning without a plan for the future, in one afternoon I had been offered a means to support myself and a way to obtain a master's degree tuition-free. It was more than I had dreamed could be possible. By the time I reached my parents' house two and a half hours later, I knew I would take the offer. It was clear the benefit was yet another form of white privilege, especially when there were so many people who needed money for education. But I had just given a year of service to America without pay, and I also knew the federal grant money was just sitting there waiting for someone like me. I reasoned that perhaps my experience with organizing could help the program. Indeed, Dr. Abdul Mu'min, a researcher in agricultural economics, had told me even my identity could perhaps help on research projects. He said he could use my help making phone calls, especially to the white farmers on our list. "I've discovered that white farmers are reluctant to respond to Black researchers, especially to someone with a Muslim name," he confided.

I had never been as conscious of my whiteness as I was during the hours I visited A&T. I knew that A&T was the university where four undergrads had staged a sit-in at the Woolworth's segregated lunch counter in downtown Greensboro, changing history. I saw the historical marker on my drive out of campus. In comparison with such acts of bravery, my privileged role in the American integration story was minuscule. Nonetheless, when the A&T opportunity fell into my lap, I believed that I should do it. At the very least, I thought, it would teach me a lot about the way America really works. Plus, earning a master's degree from a state school was no small achievement.

My two years at A&T were filled with learning and with serendipity. My initial good fortune of landing a free ride to graduate school and with a job in agricultural research to boot was followed by a series of happenstances that I look back on with deep gratitude. The first was the Rural Advancement Fund's decision to close the Graham Center and to put all of its resources into advocacy and policy work. This, in turn, led to their choice to move the organization's headquarters to the small town of Pittsboro, only half an hour or so from Raleigh, so that the staffers could lobby at the state capitol. That move put their office less than an hour from Greensboro. A second stroke of fortune was that Hope, my best friend to whom I had said good-bye at the Graham Center not knowing what our future might be, was hired to work full-time at RAF following her year as a VISTA. Third, I found out shortly after my arrival at A&T that their very short list of placement sites for student teachers—which consisted mainly of the schools where their own African American graduates taught—included Pittsboro's own Northwood High. By another stroke of good fortune, I was chosen to become the school's horticulture teacher-in-training, working under Mr. Edsel Daniel in a school only two miles from the Rural Advancement Fund office. I am not sure how much effect I had on the unruly Northwood High boys, who seemed to have been shunted off to agriculture classes to keep them in school and out of trouble; I recall only one who was interested in making horticulture his future occupation. Yet, I survived the teaching experience and learned a lot about public schools and boys in the process. But that experience fades into the background as I recall that spring, because this is the time when Hope and I fell in love.

Not long after I started teaching, RAF hired a new rural organizer, Betty Bailey, who was brought on staff to lead a new initiative called the Farm Survival Project. Sadly, right after she started her job in Pittsboro, Betty broke her arm in a fall. But her bad luck brought me good fortune: She needed a driver to shuttle her around. Hope had introduced us, and Betty, knowing I needed some extra money, asked me to help her out. After student teaching by day, I began traveling with her to meet with farmers at night. Luckily, we hit it off and worked well as a team. The help was reciprocal.

I started driving Betty's five-speed Volkswagen Rabbit in 1983. My hiring as "chauffeur" coincided with the great credit crisis during which hundreds of thousands of farmers around the nation began experiencing major financial problems. The crisis had been sparked in the 1970s when President Carter began a major grain embargo in reaction to the USSR's invasion of Czechoslovakia. Only a few years earlier, Secretary of Agriculture Earl Butz's pronouncements to "plant fencerow to fencerow" and "get big or get out" had hood-winked farmers into borrowing big and expanding their operations on credit. Having their production cut due to the embargo caused major budget shortfalls for them. The Tractorcades of the American Agriculture Movement in 1978 had shown that the dark clouds of debt were already gathering on the horizon when President Carter made his move. Some five years later when Reagan was president, these farm loans, particularly loans made by the Farmers Home Administration (FmHA), were called in, and the government became the worst offender of all the lenders. The credit crisis started to wreak havoc all over rural America, and I became the driver taking Betty to the disaster zones.

Farmers of all types began to lose land that had been in their families for generations at a rate the country had not seen since the Great Depression. RAF was the first organization in the South to step up in response. First, they sent Hope to the Center for Rural Affairs in Walthill, Nebraska, to train in how to understand the complex FmHA regulations, become a farm advocate, and set up a farmer hotline. She returned with books filled with information on farmers' rights. Soon after, RAF acquired a toll-free number and began advertising in rural newspapers to let farmers know that

RAF was standing by to help, free of charge. RAF knew from their research that thousands of farmers in the Carolinas were already facing bankruptcy or foreclosure by then, but would they call RAF's Farm Crisis Hotline? To get the word out, the organization set up a booth at the state fair, and Hope and I along with others sat together at a table and made ourselves available to talk to farmers and hand out literature to passersby. During the week of the fair, we distributed thousands of cards, brochures, and bumper stickers advertising the free service and the number. Then Hope and the others went to the office and waited near the phone.

When the first call came, Hope told me that the office was suddenly frantic. After the initial jolt, they walked the farmer through the advocacy steps, and soon after Betty set out on the road to meet with him in person. Many callers were emotionless, just people wanting information. But the hard calls also started to come in, some from wives or other family members fearing a farmer suicide. Some of the farmers threatened murder and already had a gun in the truck. Some calls came from farmers who were so far gone that the deputies had already knocked on the door and served notice of an impending sale of the family's every possession.

RAF never pretended to be a mental health service, but as the only organization responding to the crisis in the Carolinas, they got all of the calls, both tame and potentially violent. Most state agencies, be they mental health or farm-related, had not yet admitted that the rural areas were in crisis. So RAF rightly asked, "If not us, then who?" and began raising funds to do the work. Emergencies make for fast learning curves, and the small staff stepped up.

Day after day, staff members walked the callers through the lender regulations and farmers' rights as borrowers. When they felt a caller was particularly responsive, Betty would zip out in her five-speed Rabbit to meet with the farmer to talk about organizing a meeting with his or her neighbors. The initial set of responses was straightforward: First, let the calling farmer know that he or she was not alone. Second, tell the caller that this crisis was not of his or her making, but was due to structural failures in the farm economy. Third, try to encourage the caller to talk with neighbors and get them to a meeting where the RAF staff could talk with farmers about how to work together to address the problem politically. Betty, a seasoned organizer, reasoned that responding to each individual case could only be a stopgap measure to, at best, stave off a few foreclosures temporarily. Collective and structural responses through organizing, in contrast, were a strategy to change policy nationally and to save thousands of farms. Betty's plan was having some success when she broke her arm.

Given the flood of calls on its Farm Crisis Hotline, staffers had already realized they needed to hire additional help to handle the volume of calls and respond in person to the farmers in need. Betty's accident meant I had the opportunity to go to the field and demonstrate my skills at working with farmers before any position came open. By the time I graduated from A&T, I had been offered one of the positions of rural educator with RAF, a job that seemed tailored for me. I began staffing the hotline. I got my own VW diesel and began driving throughout North Carolina. I met farmers at stores, in barns, hunting lodges, volunteer fire departments, feed mills, fast-food joints, country stores, and their homes; anywhere farmers wanted to meet, I was there. Before long there were four of us, two Black men and two white, with Betty serving as our supervisor. Even with our four-fold increase in staff, there was never a shortage of work. I often returned home well past midnight having visited Lumbee, African American, and white farmers—both female and male—in over twenty counties. Though we sometimes had no immediate answers for how to help these folks and would tell them so, I had never felt so needed in my life. Our hope was that our help would lead farmers to believe they could help one another.

"You are not alone," was our common refrain for farmers everywhere. Knowing isolation was their worst enemy, our goal was to help train farmers to support one another as farmer advocates. There was no way a few of us could do all the work necessary to prop up thousands of farmers in trouble, and so our plan was to multiply our efforts. We rehashed countless times the philosophical and strategic reasons for attacking societal inequities rather than dwelling on specific individual cases. It was also good psychologically for the farmers to take the focus off themselves and help others. But our main goal was to demonstrate that political change was the only way to save family farms writ large. One analogy I used was that individual advocacy could only stop one cut from bleeding when we had thousands injured to attend to. The only way to help would be to teach others to be first responders.

In every agricultural community, regardless of race or geography, farmers' stories began at the same place: "They're taking our land and livelihood and we just want a chance to pay back our debts." Indebtedness was not even the farmers' fault for the most part. Unfair laws and credit policies that had encouraged farmers to get bigger even when they didn't want to were the real culprit. We said hundreds of times to farmers over the phone and in person, "You can't all be bad managers at once!" Most farmers who called already believed that the lenders were using this crisis as an excuse to push them out, repossess their land, and consolidate the industry into fewer hands. Most of them said, without our prompting, that the food corporations were working in cahoots with the government. With most farmers in agreement on these basic points, we believed that if farmers could just listen to one another in meetings where women and men, African Americans, Native Americans, and whites could all speak aloud about their problems, they could unite.

We started having local meetings first. We avoided becoming "outside agitators" by getting out of the way and letting farmers do the talking. We tried simply to be catalysts for conversations that farmers had already voiced individually with us on the phone. And as farmers opened up in local meetings, we became scribes, taking notes and posting salient points on butcher paper—words that seemed key to farmers' survival—for everyone to see. It was clear that most farmers at our meetings were already fighters or they wouldn't have chosen to attend to begin with. We tried to channel their fighting attitude away from raw anger and toward constructive action. They provided the will and the words. We provided listening ears, suggestions for how to run meetings, the willingness to travel to talk with others, and administrative support in setting up a network. We started feeling the pulse of rural political resurgence. But we worried whether we would we be ready when the blood pressure spiked.

Race was a major obstacle from the beginning. When Black farmers began calling the hotline to speak with us about racial discrimination, we heard firsthand how they experienced all of the mistreatment white farmers described to us. But on top of that, they were forced to confront racial barriers nearly everywhere, from loan offices to grain elevators. At FmHA loan offices, as they described them to us, their money came in the form of "supervised loans," meaning loan officers divvied out their payments one check at a time following in-person, paternalistic meetings. By contrast, more often than not, white farmers who received loans got their checks deposited directly in their own bank accounts with no questions asked. Every African American farmer we spoke with told a similar story of racial discrimination.

In light of realities that had been locked in place before the Jim Crow period, one of our greatest challenges was to convince people from every side of the color divide to engage in common work. Our initial instinct was to encourage people to unite around issues other than race when trying to forge a multiracial coalition, because to do so would garner the support of the broader public and elected officials. We thought we could encourage farmers to add a plank about overcoming racial barriers after first getting everyone to agree on common problems. This strategy was similar to one followed by the Southern Tenant Farmers' Union in the 1930s. But, for good reason, the African American farmers could not tolerate pushing race aside when this was their foremost issue. For Black farmers, postponing their core fight on race to work on common causes would have been like ignoring that their own house was on fire in order to argue about needing a better fire department for all. Gradually, we rural educators came to see they were right, but in doing so we faced a painful process of finding common ground with whites.

How could we convince white farmers to agree that dismantling racism in farm lending should be their top priority when they were also about to be foreclosed on? Even our sympathetic white leaders pleaded that we should try to save all the farms first, then tackle racism second. Black farmers replied that there could be no saving their farms without first addressing discrimination head-on. We might only get one chance at this, some Black leaders said, so we're not going to fight for family farms in general only to be forgotten about after white farmers are back in business. There was no denying that history proved them right. The arguments were painful to listen to, but we reasoned that at least we were talking about race among a mixed group of rural people in the same room.

There were, however, glimmers of reconciliation. One such moment came when an elderly Black farmer named Wilson Gerald, who had been one of the first to call the hotline when Hope answered, began a long speech about democracy in one of our integrated meetings at a volunteer fire department. With the conviction of a preacher, he spoke gently though urgently about the history of farm policy, often reciting from the Constitution and the Bible in the same paragraph. Though he didn't seem to have a pause button, and could talk for an hour before taking a breath, his status as an elder and his language kept people's attention.

"These are your United States. These are my United States," he said. "They don't belong just to the big white man. They belong to all of us. The government is made of you and me; of the people, by the people, and for the people." He spoke with the rhythm of ocean waves coming at you one after another. "Those agents down at the Farmers Home Administration work for us. We are the US government. You are the government. I am the government. And they are our employees. They need to remember that, and our elected officials need to be reminded of that, too."

We sensed right away that he was just the sort of spokesperson we needed to bring people together across racial divides, as long as we could limit his speaking time! When we asked him if he could help us get farmers to a meeting, he always delivered, including bringing white and Black farmers together to discuss their common cause. Before long, we were able to build on his local efforts. First dozens, then hundreds of farmers began coming together in county groups, volunteering to do their part to draw attention to the common plight of the tens of thousands of farmers in the Carolinas who were waiting in the shadows to see what might come of our efforts. Black farmers, who at first met mainly in their own mostly segregated communities, began talking of racial injustices before integrated groups. Some white farmers realized that Black farmers like Wilson Gerald could speak for all of them, and could actually attract audiences that they would not have had alone.

At one point we brought in Si Kahn, author of *How People Get Power*, from Charlotte as an advisor. After reading his book in college, I was elated now to be his co-worker. With his help we all found a way to help leaders of our local farmers craft a statement about fighting against racial discrimination and farm foreclosures simultaneously. The organization's platform would come to reflect much hard work and compromise. For a few seasons we maintained a united front, and our organization from the Carolinas began to stand out in national gatherings and on the news, because we were integrated and were led by women as well as men. Betty saw to it that we never swayed from our goal of equality, even when the cause had looked impossible. We just had to keep all of the farmers in the same room and talking to one another, which, of course in a racialized and divided South, was no small feat.

Charlie Thompson, with guitar, sings with UFO choir members Annie Mae Chavis, Charles Freeman, Van Scott, Jeanette King, and others. Photograph courtesy of Betty Bailey.

Gathering | *1983*

"**W**ould the United Farmers Organization chorus please come to the stage," I announced, standing at a microphone with my guitar strapped across my shoulder in a packed Ag-Expo Center auditorium in Fayetteville, North Carolina. Several elected officials would soon speak. The keynote speaker, Reverend Jesse Jackson, was standing on the floor at the corner of the stage. I had seen him speak once before, at my graduation from NC Agricultural & Technical State University, also his alma mater. This time farmers and I would be on the stage with him. After my announcement, a small procession of twelve farmers, Black and white, women and men, emerged from various points in the packed crowd and climbed the stairs to the stage, nodding to the reverend and shaking his hand as they passed. The white farmers seemed as much in awe of his leadership as the Black members.

The chorus formed a semicircle around the microphone in front of us. After I strummed an A-minor chord for the pitch, they broke into song. I had adapted the tune from one of my favorite old hymns, "I Am a Poor, Wayfaring Stranger," and turned it into a song about the farmers' plight. The original lyrics capture the very essence of the wanderer in search of a home, saying poetically, "I'm just going over home." I changed the words to echo the cause of people fighting to keep their land. The farmers had learned to sing in choirs—Black churches, white churches, all of them segregated churches—but on the stage that day in 1983, there was no distinction. All were members together, united in a quest to save their farms. This was heaven's choir as far as I was concerned.

"I am a broke, hardworking farmer!" they belted out on the first verse. The farmers had helped write some of the lines and considered the song their own. "With these hands, I work for you." You could feel their history in their handshakes. "Through these tears and toil and danger; the benefits are rich but few." They were willing to work hard, even to risk their lives in the world's second most dangerous job after mining. But they needed to be paid enough to cover their bills. Everyone needs adequate income to cover their expenses.

Then came the chorus that spoke of their commitment to work together:

> I'm not asking for a handout.
> I don't want a free ride.
> All I ask is please stand with me.
> To save these farms, side by side.

After a year of regular meetings with farmers in their communities, we had asked them to come together at the Graham Center for a two-state organizational meeting. The Rural Advancement Fund still owned the Center property at that time, though no staff worked there. It made for a good meeting place near the state line for farmers from the two Carolinas to gather, and it was free for us to use. We tried to play down the fact that it was once an organic demonstration farm. With this coalition of farmers from two states, it was more obvious than ever that farmers needed help at a much more fundamental level than VISTA volunteers showing them how to make compost. They had already voiced what they needed in their organizational meetings: emergency congressional help; nondiscriminatory lending practices; changes in the US Farm Bill; credit and debt relief; and above all, for the government to act to save an entire family farm system that had made American agriculture so successful in the first place. This, farmers agreed, would require major policy interventions in our food and farming systems.

On that Saturday at the Graham Center, farmers chose the name of their organization and elected officers. They elected Linda Clapp, a female dairy farmer, as president. George Ammons, an African American turkey farmer, was elected vice president. Tobacco, peanut, and dairy farmers formed their own commodity-based committees. Black farmers had a special caucus. Their task was to make sure issues of race stayed at the forefront of the organization's bylaws and public statements. There was much expertise on loan advocacy in the room, all gained by experience. Some of the farmers present—chicken farmer Benny Bunting among them—would go on to teach themselves the intricacies of farm credit regulations, often ending up knowing more than the lenders themselves. We had come to appreciate how much farmers knew about policy as well, especially the laws regarding the commodities they raised. They were the experts; we merely facilitated.

The farmers decided on the name United Farmers Organization (UFO), in part because they liked the whimsical sound of the initials. Their logo would be a tractor made to look like a flying saucer. But more important, they wanted the word *united* to be front and center, as it would describe the first multiracial farm group in the South since the Southern Tenant Farmers' Union. That the organization featured Black and women farmers in leadership roles made their efforts groundbreaking. No one had ever accomplished this kind of unity among diverse farm owners before. The national press noticed. Behind the scenes, ours was a delicate coalition from the beginning, but on its first day the air was electric with promise.

One of the attendees at the organizational meeting was Timothy Pigford, an African American corn and soybean farmer from eastern North Carolina whom I had visited the year before when he called the hotline. Pigford lived in a doublewide on an acre and farmed rented land. Though he was one of only a handful of young African American farmers in the state, the Farmers Home Administration— mandated in the 1930s to help both Black and white sharecroppers settle on land—now wanted him out of farming. He had told me on the phone how FmHA had treated him as though he were a child or worse. He described what being talked down to felt like. While white farmer neighbors who applied for loans later than he did received their loans right away, his operating money never came. Then after years of crop losses caused in part by the lender, FmHA told him they were closing him out and would soon come for his equipment. He decided to call our Farm Crisis Hotline, and then to fight for change. He would go on to lead the UFO as a champion of endangered Black farmers across the South. His case against the FmHA later became a class action lawsuit, now famously known as *Pigford v. Glickman*, the defendant being Dan Glickman, the US secretary of agriculture at the time. The suit would be brought by one of our organizational allies, the nonprofit Farmers' Legal Action Group (FLAG) from St. Paul, Minnesota.

On its first day, the UFO voted to join with other organizations in calling for a moratorium on all FmHA farm foreclosures nationwide. With the farmers' widespread coalition demanding attention, Congress responded affirmatively and held off on foreclosures for twenty-five months. Numerous individual cases of our members went into appeal and, at times with neighbors supporting them with signs and chants outside loan offices, we won back their right to farm. Meanwhile, the RAF staff produced several publications on farmers' rights and specifically how to negotiate in loan hearings.

As a response to the UFO requests for help, Congressman Charlie Rose called the entire Agriculture Committee from the US House of Representatives to Fayetteville, North Carolina, for our first regional hearing. At our second large gathering in North Carolina, Reverend Jesse Jackson lent his support. He took the stage after the UFO choir sang the last verse of their theme song:

> Now they want to come and take it.
> All these years of toil and sweat.
> But with my neighbors standing with me,
> I can say, you ain't got it yet!

Reverend Jackson commented on the power in the room as he took the stage and looked out at the diverse audience. He took our excitement up a notch from there, exactly as we had hoped, as he preached about the meaning of family farms for democracy. He talked about how race and economics are intertwined, echoing his mentor Dr. King. We applauded until our hands hurt, and then our choir sang again. A national family farm movement had begun and the media showed we were part of it. Farmers read their own statements, which we had helped type up, to eager reporters from around our states and beyond. Our movement echoed the 1930s Farm Holiday movement in the Midwest. The Tractorcades of the American Agriculture Movement had also planted seeds of action. Now the UFO was helping nurture the sprouts that resulted.

A few years later in 1985, Willie Nelson, John Mellencamp, and Neil Young, one of my longtime favorite singer-songwriters, would join forces with farmers for the first Farm Aid concert. Afterward, our farmers would take part in widespread organizational meetings made possible by the musicians' fund-raising network. Farm Aid helped distribute cash to needy rural families and hay to farmers experiencing drought. RAF and UFO members were present for national trainings held by FLAG. When we sent a farmer named Charlie Bouldin to meet backstage with Willie Nelson, he returned to start a concert series in his own community: a weekly Friday night barn dance held on his dairy farm.

We took Black and white farmers together to national meetings, and that made us different. Though I had heard farmers say perhaps hundreds of times, "You can't organize farmers," I always made a point of telling them they were just repeating a cliché, as typically they said it as part of a group of farmers already gathered in the same room. And the most gratifying scenes for me were seeing people of completely different backgrounds working together toward common goals. We witnessed farmers crossing boundaries the cynics said could never be crossed. Thus, during the years UFO stayed together, we did make change, not only in the courts and in Congress, but in the hearts and minds of our members as well. National as well as local leaders emerged from our group. Many testified multiple times before Congress. Others became lay legal experts. And perhaps most important, farmers learned to share their stories aloud with one another, saving some from slipping into depression and perhaps even suicide.

Then, like plants that grow vigorously for a time only to wither and die as the winter sets in, the UFO had its seasons of productivity and then waned and atrophied. We had found common cause for a while. Then in the late 1980s, some of our more establishment-oriented white farmers received their loans and decided, as predicted, they were no longer interested in being part of a controversial group as it could jeopardize those loans. And with change coming too slowly, some of our African American farmer leaders decided they had to put their energies into saving Black land as their sole focus. Statistics at the time showed that all Black farmers could be gone by the year 2000, and waiting was impossible. By 1990 some of our Black farmer members, who would go on to organize the national class action lawsuit, set out on their own. When one of our own Black co-workers left to help them, the leadership of the UFO decided to disband rather than watch their numbers dwindle.

But how could we not be proud of the work they had done while together? We had, for a while at least, crossed barriers long in the making. Even if we had not dismantled racial boundaries for all time, people of diverse backgrounds had stood together side by side. In the end, we had to admit that the legacy of our country's racist history could not be undone quickly. Change comes in increments. The leaders of the Southern Tenant Farmers' Union knew they were building on the prior work of others when they gathered in the 1930s. Civil rights leaders knew it when they marched in the 1960s. Dr. King knew it when he gave his speech to the sanitation workers in Memphis just before his assassination. All of us knew deep down when we started organizing the UFO that we would not finish the work, and that our goals would take generations to achieve. I, like everyone who has ever worked for social change, had to conclude that we stand on the shoulders of others who came before us, and that we are not about to end the struggle on our watch, either.

Seeds of change the UFO planted have continued bearing fruit to this day. Following the moratorium, Congress mandated new lending practices and even lasting changes to the US Farm Bill. Farmer advocates who trained during our organization's heyday—some of them now in their eighties—are still helping save farms today. The old guard has also trained younger people who comprise new generations of advocates in national networks still sponsored by Farm Aid. Countless farm families remain in business because of the individual advocacy our farmers fostered. Some are on their land today because UFO members refused to go quietly. In 2010, under the guidance of Attorney General Eric Holder of the Obama administration, payments won in the *Pigford v. Glickman* lawsuit finally made it to some thirty-four thousand African American families who had waited decades to receive them, twenty-five years after FLAG had won the case at the Supreme Court.

Justice work taught me that building community-based groups has much in common with farming. Even knowing there is a very good chance of a crop failure each season, we plant believing our work will bear fruit, if not now, then sometime, somewhere. Farmers' uncanny optimism keeps them returning to sow seeds in fallow ground, even after droughts or when storms cut down their crops in their prime. Justice work is born of that same spirit. We keep believing in humanity's ability to change, even during the times when we cannot see past today's news.

Jean Wynot, farmer and hotline operator, helping a farmer client with his loan papers, Lawndale, North Carolina, 1988. Photograph by Rob Amberg.

Reseeding | *1984*

No farmer I have ever listened to or championed—no matter his or her age or region—talked about working the land without mentioning a relative, often many generations of kin, who farmed before them. Sometimes African American farmers' memories touched on ancestor stories that harked back to slavery. Some Black farmers as well as whites talked of family members who had worked their way out of indentured servitude or sharecropping to landownership. Native American tenure on the land reaches back to the beginning of agriculture on this continent, and diverse tribal nations tell as many stories of loss and regrowth as anyone on the planet. Regardless of background, no farmer ever claimed to me that he or she was self-made.

Since childhood, I have always loved farming stories. In my work as an organizer, I began writing down farmers' words, of joy as well as pain and loss, sometimes helping farmers turn their stories into letters that they mailed to congresspersons. I helped them prepare their statements for loan hearings. I copied and rewrote them for spoken testimonies before elected officials. Steeped in farmers' words, I heard echoes of love from my own ancestors whose words I have carried inside me from childhood. I came to see that stories are the bedrock that people stand on when they fight against the odds. I started keeping these sayings down in a notebook.

I once met with a father-son duo with the last name Sholar in Duplin County, North Carolina, on the farm that had been in their family for over a century. We stood in a cornfield near the barn where they raised broiler chickens for a small processing plant owned by a single family that had recently succumbed to foreclosure because it could not compete with the big integrators. When Watson's Poultry closed their doors, dozens of farmers were suddenly left with no market for their chickens. Workers in the plant lost their jobs. My task was to help these people strategize about how to save their community. The father on this small farm, Wayne Sholar, and his son E. B., emerged as leaders in our campaign. The three of us were meeting to strategize about legal matters one day when Wayne paused and began to talk about why he cared about his family's place. He shared a memory from when his family used only manure for fertilizer and most every chore had been done by hand.

"I was working with my family one day," he began. "I was standing with a pitchfork on the back of a honey [manure] wagon. And I had gotten strong enough to where I could sling manure right down through those rows of corn. I was like a musician strumming his strings, real smooth and easy-like." He had painted a poetic scene of a boy learning to work with his family, remembering the satisfaction of doing a job well among people he loved. That particular quote went straight to my heart and changed me. After hearing so many words from so many farmers and plant workers, that was the one that broke down my defenses. I wanted to fall to my knees in the field and cry "uncle" right then. So many people, so many stories, and now this simple, almost innocent line was the one that reached into me so deep.

My job was to help this family and all their neighbors fight for their right to a livelihood. To do that I had to call on the same irrational optimism that had made me dream of farming even in the midst of family loss. Even if I wanted to crumple, I had to keep standing in that field trying to help the Sholars hold on to what they had, even though I knew the odds were against them. If I had not believed in fighting for farmers to begin with, I wouldn't have taken such a job. Somehow that crazy belief in people working the soil kept me going even when I wanted to quit. And then that sense of purpose made me do a crazy thing like imagining a farm of my own in the midst of the worst economic crisis since the Great Depression.

"You mean even after hearing about all the toil and danger that we've been through and sung about, you still want to be a farmer?" asked Charles Freeman, one of my closest farmer friends in the UFO, and a singer in the choir. He was quoting from our song to chide me, to warn me that this vocation was never easy, but especially then.

I trusted Charles, especially after he showed his gentle side when he sang. He would tilt back his two-toned head—the lower part permanently scorched red by the sun, and the pale upper part always covered by a farm cap, except in church—and, with his eyes closed, belt out the lyrics of our songs. But I also knew he was a fighter who had no qualms about talking back to loan officers or the powerful landowners in his county on behalf of the many they had pushed off their property. He was on the front line when we protested fore-closures. He was white, but he was also a close friend and neighbor of Wilson Gerald, and he was willing to stand with him and other people of color in public, and show his unity with them on issues of racial equity. He had lost several fingers on his right hand in a farm machinery accident, but that was only a small inconvenience compared with his outsized personality and large laugh. When he shook hands with others, he gripped with his few remaining fingers, showing his farmer's spirit. I had figured he would challenge me when I told him about my farming ambitions, and that was one reason I told him. But I also knew he would see why I wanted to farm. "I guess every farmer has to be a little crazy," he said.

I looked back at him with a sheepish smile, and admitted, "Believe it or not, I want to try to get a beginning farmer loan from our friends at the FmHA!" Though I knew that Charles and so many others had gone through hell at the government lending agency, he and I shared a mission to change the agency. I wasn't applying because I thought myself superior to other farmers undergoing hardship, or to prove a political point; deep down I really wanted to farm for a living and believed the government should help people. From my close reading of the regulations, I knew I qualified as a "begin-ning farmer." People like Wilson Gerald and Charles Freeman had shown me why it is good to believe in agriculture *and* the American government, and to insist they (who are really "we," as Mr. Gerald would say) do the right thing. It is easy to give in to cynicism and say the government will never help the little people. But pessimism has no place in farming. Farming, more than any other occupation, is about believing in the unseen, in the will of a seed to push from darkness into light.

I also knew that even though we had won a few battles, small family farmers were losing the war. Thanks to federal farm policies that favored industrial agriculture, agribusiness was racking up victories everywhere in America. To them, people I had worked with like Charles Freeman, Wilson Gerald, and Annie Mae Chavis were chaff to be blown away so the real producers could step up their production. Their trajectory made my quest to get into the farming business during such an economic crisis both ludicrous and necessary at the same time.

After working with so many of the survivors of farm losses, I knew that we had to build an alternative movement and help invent a new family farm system that would be fairer to people. I knew that might mean starting almost from scratch. But the answer was not to quit and admit defeat. Even Thoreau, with his rejection of the American economy writ large and his critique of the farmers around him, still planted beans. He complained of farms owning people, but still he committed himself to growing and harvesting crops he raised. In that spirit, I wanted to devise a farm plan that would allow me to work with the soil as a tangible reflection of both justice and tradition. My goal would be to provide a model that could be given to farmers in trouble. But first I would have to face a lender that I knew was not on my side.

My dream farm would have to be small and close enough to markets so that I could engage directly in them, because cutting out the middleman allows producers to charge prices they can survive on. It would be centered on local sales of organic fruits and vegetables; our main crops would be perennials: blackberries, blueberries, apples, and asparagus. These I would supplement with annual vegetables and strawberries. Lamb and perhaps even some organic beef could be added later. I would rely on building relationships with consumers who enjoyed working with groups of farmers, and combine pick-your-own sales with deliveries to restaurants and grocery stores, becoming profitable while simultaneously building community. Instead of buying their produce in sterile packages from anonymous sources, my customers could shake my hand and get to know me (and I would get to know them). We would emphasize regeneration, meaning that the land and the people who worked it would receive sustenance directly from the work and the relationships it fostered. Most important, because people should be able to pass on their farms to others for many generations to come, we would make a place where children could play safely and learn.

Though we were not yet married, Hope and I had begun to talk about owning a farm together. She would help with farm chores when possible, but would keep her full-time job at RAF. I would also keep my job for a while, and then gradually move into production full-time. All we needed to start, I believed, was some land with a simple house on it. With our jobs, we thought we could make it without having to borrow operating money. But we did need an ownership loan, particularly one that provided a low interest rate that I could pay back over the coming decades without undue financial strain—exactly the kind of loan FmHA had been mandated to provide decades before I was born. I knew as well as anyone the reason for the agency's existence. I had studied the Rural Resettlement Administration's lofty goals. Unfortunately, I had also discovered how they had changed over the decades. I knew how the loan officers treated the growers they held in low esteem. For those reasons and more, I knew my chances as a small farmer would be slim. At the same time, I knew I had a congressional mandate on my side. If they denied me a beginning loan, we could fight it all the way to Washington. I believed in this cause wholeheartedly.

Pittsboro, where RAF had located, was only twenty miles from Chapel Hill, the home of the University of North Carolina, which, I reasoned, had a growing population of educated faculty and students who likely understood some of the challenges farmers faced. It made sense to look for land near such a clientele, so I began searching nearby. On the first day, our realtor friend, Elizabeth Anderson, took me to visit a worn-out tobacco farm just two miles south of Pittsboro. The farm, which once encompassed several hundred acres, had been whittled down by single-family housing and a new road to just twenty-two acres, less than a fifth of its original size. But the remaining land at least had a house, a pond, and a few outbuildings, which made it a more livable farm than most other parcels on the market.

The most recent farmers to own the property were a retired couple who owned a few horses. They had purchased the place from the Fawcett family who had raised tobacco on the land for several generations, and who sold the farm when the grandmother died. The new owners had made improvements, and the place was starting to rejuvenate when the husband was tragically killed after running into a nest of hornets on his tractor. Under duress, his widow put the farm on the market immediately. It sold to a dentist in Raleigh who owned over ninety rental houses. After purchasing the farm, Dr. Radnor rented out the old house to nonfarming tenants, and the land remained idle, growing up in broom sedge and small pines.

When Elizabeth and I pulled into the driveway, I noticed the fences had fallen over, and even the house and outbuildings had started to decay. To spruce up the house for sale, the dentist's maintenance workers had spray-painted the entire house gray, even covering the outer edges of the window glass. The interior was covered with old corrugated cardboard washing machine boxes that had been painted white to look like sheetrock. Every room was carpeted with the same cheap maroon shag. The once-high farmhouse ceilings had been dropped to seven feet with insulation board, making the rooms feel claustrophobic. Later that week I took a contractor friend to see the place. He advised me to tear the house down and start anew if I bought the farm.

But there were still signs of beauty. The horse farmer had built a little red barn out behind the house. There were good hardwood trees, including six stately white oaks that shaded the old home. These remnants of its farming past drew me to the place even though the house and the fields were uninspiring. After surveying what I thought was the whole property, I looked up the hill above the house and said, "If only that field up there could be added to the farm, I would be more interested." Then I looked down again at the plat and description Elizabeth had given me, and I realized that the field, measuring nearly five acres, *was* on the map, despite it being left off of the originating realtor's description. Elizabeth hadn't noticed the oversight. With the addition of that field, I saw that the house was situated in middle of the property rather than relegated to the edge. The little farm now seemed in balance visually, and I was instantly more intrigued, especially because the upper field appeared flat and more fertile. I practically ran up the hill so I could kick around in the soil and find out.

As I had hoped, the land on top of the hill did have loamy soil that had not eroded away. It would be enough to start, and I told Elizabeth I wanted to consider buying the place. Cautioning my enthusiasm, Elizabeth said her next step would be to verify the exact outer perimeter, and then to talk with the dentist to see if he would be willing to wait for me to secure a farm loan, which she knew was a long shot. What incentive would the dentist have for keeping the land off the market while I negotiated with the government? Would someone like him understand the FmHA's mandate? Would he see the larger picture of farm histories and society's need to preserve rural land and its farmers? If he were just a housing mogul, I had no reason even to try to convince him.

Sensing that without a personal connection to the land or to me, there would be no chance he would wait, I decided to make an appointment to talk directly with Dr. Billy Radnor at his real estate office in Raleigh. On the surface, I found Radnor to be a brusque man better typecast as a slumlord than a dentist, but as we talked, his demeanor changed. He, too, had once loved his grandparents' farm, he said. But he was also frustrated with trying to sell this particular place. One sale had already fallen through, he said, and added, "I don't like owning farmland as rental property anyway." He wanted tenants on urban small-town lots, ones that his full-time maintenance men wouldn't have to spend so much time on. I didn't ask if they had been the ones to install the cardboard and carpet, but I assumed so. Knowing that my chances were slim, I explained the challenges of acquiring farm loans and about the FmHA program for beginning farmers. He listened impatiently, as if he had somewhere else to be.

After I had my say, I stood to leave, thanking him for his time, still not knowing what he really thought of my plan. I had reached for the door when he said, "I'll wait on your loan application. I may not seem like I care about that kind of thing, but I hope your plan will work out for you." I turned to thank him and told him I would work as hard as possible to make this quick, but so much was out of my hands. I told him that my realtor would be back with a contract to purchase as soon as possible. I didn't know what the FmHA might require, I told him, but hopefully the forms would be standard. "That sounds fine," he replied. Then he blurted out as I pushed open the storm door, "I just want you to know that if your loan doesn't make, I'm going to turn the whole place into a trailer park." I swallowed hard, trying to show no emotion, and nodded. I knew he was serious. I believed I could trust him to wait at least a while, but I left without a signed agreement. Now the stakes riding on that little, worn-out piece of ground and a government loan were clear: The future of the farm itself depended on my single application.

Of course, I knew all the reasons my FmHA application could be shot down. I knew how stacked against me the deck was before I walked into the loan office. I knew the North Carolina office had made very few beginning farm ownership loans in the last decade. And worse, I understood that our County Committee—a ruling farm junta of just two good old boys—would determine my fate. Following the weak opening hand my farm history had dealt me, they would play their ineligibility card—the most powerful in the deck, as we have already seen.

Hope Shand and Charlie Thompson, with Gulf Coast Native Sheep.
Photograph by Rob Amberg.

Raising | *1984*

*A*fter receiving the letter of rejection from the County Committee at FmHA, I wrote a six-page letter missive titled, "Response to the Unfavorable Decision." The document, intended for my official file, opened with the following lines:

> Small farmers are in trouble. Without new ways of approaching farming and marketing, they are destined for extinction. My plan is a model for small farms in this area. . . . My plan and preparation are sound. . . . I taught agriculture at Northwood High School last year. I work with small farmers now. . . . [But] one obstacle for new farmers in this area is credit.

I concluded five pages later with this question:

> If someone with my credentials is not allowed into farming with a plan that will make money, who will be farming in the year 2000?

I hand-delivered this response to the new county supervisor, Kenny Hill, along with a copy of my revised eight-page farm plan and supporting letters written by farmers, the county extension agent, the NC State berry specialist, as well as the official forms required by the lender. I asked Mr. Hill to treat this as new evidence and to place the packet in my file. Then I formally requested, based on the new evidence, that the County Committee entertain the application a second time. A week or so later, I received a second letter of rejection stating:

> Based solely on the information we now have on file, we found no substantial reason for another County Committee review for reconsideration at this time.

The letter continued with several clauses about my possible failure to meet certain criteria for loan eligibility and their needing further income statements, balance sheets, pro forma income statements, and other information. Then the letter concluded with standard instructions on how to appeal this second decision to the state level. There was no question that I would. As instructed in the guidelines, I wrote Hill to request this next step.

Right away, I asked a few allies to attend the hearing with me, including Mark Epp, my former supervisor at the Graham Center; Bill Dow, a local community organizer and organic grower; and Hope, who was both a farm advocate and, by then, my fiancée. I procured additional letters of endorsement. Hope and I joked about whether we should call upon my United Farmers Organization friends to protest outside the hearing room, though the last thing I wanted to do was to appear to use my RAF work for my own benefit. I could only imagine what the FmHA would do with that. At the same time, we all knew mine was part of a larger political fight for the agricultural justice we believed in.

Bill, who never pulled punches, said as we stood outside the meeting room door, "I hope they deny you. I want to take this all the way to Washington." He thought we could use my case to prove officially that small-scale organic agriculture was a legitimate farming practice. "I agree with you in principle," I said, "But I'm sure I don't want to be the 'poster child' for a national fight." My real goal was to farm, not just prove a point. He laughed as we walked into a second-floor room of the Wake County Courthouse in Raleigh and took our seats.

It was February. Already four months had elapsed since I had talked with Dr. Radnor and submitted my first application. Though expecting the worst, I decided to remain as positive as possible. "Don't lose your temper," I repeated to myself. FmHA had three people present: Mr. Hill, the county supervisor; a hearing officer named James Kearney, who had been appointed by the state director; and a stenographer who took handwritten notes and recorded the conversation on cassette tape. I was pleasantly surprised that I did not recognize Mr. Kearney, and that he was African American. Not that race guaranteed sympathy with small farmers, but I reasoned that if anyone on the inside of the agency could still believe in the original mission of the FmHA, hopefully a person of color would be a good candidate. The hearing opened with Mr. Kearney stating the points of the original committee's decision, followed by Mr. Hill giving a brief history of the denial. Then it was my turn to speak.

The transcript of the hearing states that I began talking about my grandparents' farm, and then mentioned that my parents were living near them and farming with them part-time. I spoke of my experience in Georgia where I "worked in a large market-size garden," as well as the Graham Center, where I "managed a demonstration garden." I continued, "I also taught agriculture at Northwood High School as student teacher, and now I work with Rural Advancement Fund." I then proceeded with my explanation of a marketing plan and my presentation of letters of support, brochures, articles about berry farming, and a statement from the NC A&T Research Farm where I had worked. I concluded by saying that there had been a misunderstanding with the County Committee. They couldn't have known how well I was prepared for this venture, I argued. "I would have liked to have had the opportunity to be heard by the County Committee so we could have cleared this up," the recorder quoted my words in her notes.

Then Mark asked a crucial question at exactly the right time: "Why was the plan being considered usual or unusual used as a point of denial, when it is not part of the criteria that Mr. Thompson must meet?" Based on the agency's own rules, Mr. Hill had to acquiesce: "That is correct, whether a farm is usual or unusual is not one of the criteria," he said. Mark said, "Thank you," knowing he had found a crucial chink in the agency's armor.

Mr. Kearney then asked me a series of questions. "What were the alternative uses of the twenty-two acres of land?" I stated that the owner said the property would become a trailer park if my loan were denied. Then he followed with, "Do you have any alternatives to owning the land?" I replied that a lease agreement would not work with perennial crops. Having land for an extended period of time was crucial. Then he revealed that the agency was privy to my advocacy work. "Is there any connection between your request and the efforts of the Rural Advancement Fund?" I answered that there was no professional or financial relationship between the farm in question and the organization. The recorder wrote down every word. I was so glad at that moment there wasn't a group of farmers singing the UFO theme song outside the window! The FmHA had to have known about RAF, but they were being as careful as I was. The hearing ended amicably. I had kept my temper and everyone on my team had been on their best behavior. There was some reason for optimism as we descended the stairs.

I was forced to wait a month before receiving their decision in the mail. When the letter finally arrived, this time I ripped it open immediately. It was signed by the state director. The envelope was thick because it included the transcript of the hearing and other documents. I braced myself for the first paragraph of the cover letter. I felt my chest swell as I got to the third line, "We have made the decision to reverse the action of the County Committee." But then, as if to deflate any undue elation, the underlined next sentence stated: "This does not mean in any way that a loan will be approved for you." Dr. Radnor and I had waited nearly six months only to learn that I was now eligible to apply. But this letter meant I had bypassed the County Committee, and now the loan officer, Mr. Kenny Hill, would have the authority to decide on the loan. He, of course, was a bureaucrat who shied away from giving me any outward indication of whether or not he supported the farm idea, but at least he appeared to have no vendetta against me.

At my appointment the following week, Mr. Hill told me that when one of the members of the County Committee learned of the reversal of their decision—likely their first experience of the sort—that member said in anger, "You'll never get a dime of your money back if you make that loan." They just didn't like your plan, Hill said. But then he tacked on this curious addendum: "But if you had applied for a loan for a chicken farm, you would have probably gotten a loan right away."

Incredulous, I asked, "You mean FmHA would have loaned me hundreds of thousands of dollars to start a [commercial] chicken operation on the same land?" He replied, "Probably, because that's a typical farm for the area and a lot of people are going into it and making money." It didn't seem to matter that I had no experience running large-scale chicken houses. I was also appalled that the agency would so blatantly support corporate farms over individual entrepreneurship. But I knew this was not the place or time to discuss farm politics, including how large poultry conglomerates often cut the contracts of farmers just as their loans were due, particularly those who questioned the management recommendations made by company representatives. I also had to hold my tongue about the dozens of farmers I knew who had been left without chickens and deeply in debt, some of them now calling our hotline.

Benny Bunting, our UFO poultry and farm loan expert—one who had lost his contract—had uncovered numerous abuses within the industry all across the South. We had heard dozens of corroborating stories from poultry farmers at our meetings, though they were too vulnerable to say anything in public. It wasn't clear who was treated worse: the confined chickens or the farmers who grew them. Also, a few months before I met with Mr. Hill, I had visited with John and Mary Clouse, whose farm was not three miles from Radnor's place. They told me they weren't getting chickens to raise that year even though their production record had been impeccable. They suspected they were cut off because they had talked back to the company's representative. Or maybe it was their membership in the UFO.

John had been in charge of a substation in Micronesia for NASA as a communications technician for the Apollo missions. He also had extensive experience with animal husbandry growing up on his family's farm in Kansas. He could have run the entire poultry company in his sleep. Mary was a former teacher in the Peace Corps in Africa, a trained bookkeeper, and had also grown up in rural America. I had never met a more articulate farm couple. Everyone who knew the Clouses loved them and understood how overqualified they were to raise birds under contract. But the company had the gall to tell them they were being let go because of their lack of management ability.

After knowing chicken farmers like the Clouses personally, I wouldn't have touched a contract with a poultry integrator with a grant, much less a loan. Plus, since I believed chicken farming in large confinement units to be the epitome of an unsustainable, chemical-intensive, contractual arrangement that is bad for farmers, consumers, the birds, the land, and the neighbors of chicken farms—the polar opposite of my ideals—there was no way I would have considered such a loan. But I could have gotten it anyway, said FmHA.

Despite our obvious differences of opinion about how to address the ill health of farming in general, Mr. Hill and I did establish a good rapport over the next few months. And he came through for me and I got the loan. Plus, miraculously, Dr. Radnor waited for their decision. Late in the spring of 1984, nine months after I first walked over the farm and saw a diamond in the rough, I handed the government check to Elizabeth, who got all of the papers signed and the check delivered to Radnor, and I became a farm borrower at age twenty-eight. My entry into agriculture would represent but a tiny blip upward on an otherwise depressing graph showing the falling number of farmers nationwide. But at least now I had a chance to prove my plan would work.

That evening Hope and I walked over the land and talked and dreamed. By nightfall, she had gone back to her little house in town, and I started burning brush I had cleared from the overgrown fencerow. While I tended the fire, a rare whippoorwill sang its unceasing song in the dark woods nearby. Until then, I had only heard these nocturnal birds in the mountains of Virginia. Hearing it there in the middle of the Piedmont on that auspicious first evening of our farm ownership seemed a welcoming sign from nature itself. I drove back to Hope's house that night and told her why I felt Whippoorwill Farm might make a good farm name. She liked it instantly, and the name stuck.

Charlie Thompson selling at his Carrboro Farmers' Market stand in 1986.

Harvesting | *1985*

*E*verything that I had ever learned about farms over the years, from my first memories with my grandparents to my recent fieldwork with UFO farmers, seemed to burst into bloom all at once; I had never felt so motivated to work as I did on Whippoorwill Farm. I began putting in fourteen-hour days without fail. I woke up early and was at the farm before reporting to RAF. I was there every night after returning home. I worked by headlights or moonlight, often past midnight.

After clearing brush, I built fences, laid irrigation pipes, and started to plant asparagus, blueberry bushes, and fruit trees. I used every hour of my weekends to try to catch the cool days of the burgeoning spring. After dark, carpenter friends helped me renovate the house, tearing out the old carpet and cardboard. We stripped the walls down to the studs, and the ceiling and flooring to the joists. When Hope left town to work for a four-month sabbatical at Jubilee Partners—an offshoot of Koinonia, whose main mission was to help Central American refugees—I set to work even harder, sometimes only sleeping six hours a night. I was nest building and we knew it.

After Hope and I married the summer of 1985, we decided I could soon go into farming full-time and she became a co-borrower. As I left RAF, we built a greenhouse, planted more acreage in fruits and vegetables, started raising hay, and bought a starter flock of sheep. We also bought a small tractor and a tractor-mounted tiller for making raised beds. I borrowed a neighbor's dump truck and front-end loader to haul in tons of mulch and manure. I added at least a hundred tons of organic matter to that place the first year, and slowly the land began to come alive.

A year later I began selling at the Carrboro Farmers' Market in Chapel Hill, just as consumer demand for organic and local food started increasing exponentially. After a modest start, I began to learn the art of planting for markets. Before long I was packing up a truck, and sometimes both a full truck and trailer, and selling everything I could grow. Just as I had outlined in my FmHA farm plan, blackberries and blueberries became my main offerings, with three seasons of vegetables—spring, summer, and fall—filling in around those. On Friday nights, Hope and I sometimes stayed up at times past two a.m. washing and bagging greens and even making salad dressing featuring our own labels. I was heading to market by four thirty, knowing I had to have everything arranged by six a.m. to accommodate the early-bird customers. A few years later, I was elected to the board of the market, just as our market became nationally known as a leader in grower-controlled markets and was written up in numerous publications.

Around the same time, my former RAF colleague Betty joined the North Carolina Council of Churches Rural Life Committee, and the group began planning to organize farmers markets in church parking lots. They invited me to attend a meeting, and a week or so later she called to ask if I would lead their new project, "Seeds of Hope Farmers' Markets." Their goal was to organize new farmer-controlled markets in small towns and urban church parking lots. It was clear how much farmers needed the sales outlets, as we had started turning away growers at Carrboro already. I had also witnessed the growing demand for local goods all across the state. I accepted the position and began spending my winter months and rainy days making phone calls and hitting the road, again, to find both the growers and market locations. It was a feel-good campaign for everyone. Who could be against buying local produce directly from farmers?

A year after I began organizing Seeds of Hope markets, the state of North Carolina opened a major new State Farmer's

Market in Raleigh. The infamous agriculture commissioner, Jim Graham—nicknamed, by some, the Sodfather—had considered the eighteen-million-dollar facility one of his proudest accomplishments, a kind of crowning glory to his long career in public office. When he wore his cowboy hat and chewed on a cigar for the ribbon cutting that spring, all the news seemed positive, with state leaders celebrating the North Carolina Department of Agriculture (NCDA) for its service to the state. However, knowing that the NCDA had a reputation for fostering agribusiness, particularly big tobacco, I was skeptical.

Not long after the big facility opened, I suddenly had way too many blackberries to sell at my regular outlets, so I decided to take my extra flats to the state market to see if I could try wholesaling them. Upon arrival, a man at the entrance directed me to the fresh produce shed instead. I drove by dozens of semis unloading their wares and then got out of the truck. Carrying two of my flats, I walked up to two different farm stand sellers at their booths to talk about my berries. After taking a look at the berries, the two bought my whole load between them and both paid me in cash on the spot. It was too quick. That transaction would have been against our markets' cardinal rules of growing what you sell. They never even asked me who I was or where I lived. They didn't seem to care. I walked away with cash in my pocket, glad to find a home for the berries, but I felt strange about the transaction.

As I drove back to the farm to prepare my next delivery, I began to question why millions of our tax dollars seemed to be helping "middlemen" who buy from other growers, while I was out peddling my own goods and driving around the state trying to find church parking lots where struggling small farmers could sell. Were our tax dollars really helping farmers who needed assistance? I brought up that question in my report at the next Rural Life Committee meeting. The members, many of them pastors, encouraged me to write an op-ed piece about what had happened. I wrote the article, and a member of our committee sent it out to a syndicated group that in turn distributed it to papers all around the state. In the editorial, I charged that our own agriculture department appeared to be creating unfair competition by referring to people who buy and resell produce "local growers." I argued that the term "local" must have strict guidelines, as with our grower-controlled markets.

The Sodfather was livid. Commissioner Graham saw my criticism of his market as a personal affront and began his counterattack. The week the op-ed appeared, one of his assistants called up the Council of Churches Rural Life Committee chairperson, Reverend Joe Mann, and warned, "If this doesn't stop, someone is going to get hurt." I received a call later the same week from a different assistant who said the same thing to me directly on my home phone. Meanwhile, the column continued trickling out in weekly papers all around the state, out of my control at that point. Every day seemed to bring a new small-town reprinting. I was elated and scared at the same time. Scared because I *did* have something to lose in this game. And besides, what did the Sodfather's minions mean exactly by "someone is going to get hurt"?

The following Saturday I went through my regular routine of selling at our Carrboro Farmers' Market. Without my being aware of it, our manager, Chester Copeland, was approached by the manager of the Raleigh State Market who happened to also be named Charlie, like me. As far as Chester knew, this was Charlie's first visit to our market. According to Chester, the distinguished visitor tried to sound as nonchalant as possible: He just happened to be in the neighborhood and wanted to take some pictures. "Would you mind if I walk around with my camera?" he asked politely. When Chester gave him permission, which was only a formality anyway, Charlie proceeded toward my stand, stood behind a post, and took pictures of me and my produce for over an hour.

"He stood right over yonder," Chester told me a week later. "And he took pictures just of you the whole time. You were too busy to look up to see him. I wanted to tell you, but I was also busy that morning, and I thought maybe he was going to do an article on you or something." I thanked Chester and told him not to worry about it.

Now what was I supposed to do? I had nothing to hide. I had grown every flower, potato, squash, or berry I sold. Even my farm scale hanging in plain view had been inspected by the state. Yet, here were state officials who were supposedly minding the farmers' business coming after me. Was this an intimidation tactic, or were they preparing to try something? For the next month, I feared that I could see inspectors from the NCDA drive into our farm and attempt to shut it down. Part of me hoped they would try. But I also knew they had numerous staff attorneys at their disposal who could make mincemeat out of my challenge. It was all a good reminder why organizing is the best approach to making change. Groups provide some protection. Acting alone begets vulnerability.

I did have one trick up my sleeve, however: I told one of my early-bird customers, who happened to be the former president of the University of North Carolina system, about the phone calls and the photographs. Dr. William Friday, one of the most respected citizens in the state and who regularly appeared on public television, listened intently. Then he replied, "I taught Jim Graham at NC State back when he was just a boy. If he does anything, you tell me. I'll have a talk with him."

While that reassurance helped immeasurably, a year or more passed before I stopped looking over my shoulder for a white truck with the green NCDA insignia to drive in and ask to inspect our fields or our scale or something with which the department could harass me. In the end, I began telling the story to my friends, laughing a little about being pursued by the Sodfather himself. I was glad I had written the piece, and I was elated as the story resulted in pastors from churches all over the state meeting officials at the Raleigh market and asking some hard questions.

★ ★ ★

Meanwhile, production at Whippoorwill Farm continued to grow each week. I began selling at two markets, along with making deliveries to restaurants and grocery stores twice a week. This yielded enough money to start hiring high school students as part-time help; even in what I had considered off-months, I stayed busy with greenhouses and animal production. Being the president of the Carrboro market took additional time. By the winter of my second year at Seeds of Hope, I decided to turn over the reins of the organization to Susan Vickery, a young woman I had hired to assist me. By the third spring, the farm was beginning to pay its bills, and we were able to get a little ahead of schedule on paying back the FmHA ownership loan. Of course, this was only possible because our health insurance and other off-farm expenditures were paid through Hope's job, but that had been the plan all along. Gradually the farm was starting to be the model of a successful organic farm we had hoped it would be.

At the same time, we knew that our success stemmed, in part, from being only twenty miles from Chapel Hill, where we could ride the wave of interest in buying local and organic from its affluent university community. We were lucky that our customers knew exactly why they wanted to go out of their way to buy from us. Taste was paramount, but so were the politics of local buying. Our customers were willing to pay more for food from growers they could trust, and they were also hoping to push back against food marketing trends that favored the large over the small. Because we sold to the same customers week after week, we built lasting relationships with people who knew their dollars were supporting our farm directly. Customers began to line up to buy from us, and some even followed me home to buy meats directly from our freezer—all of it processed in state government-inspected plants, of course!

There were also encouraging signs among our more traditional growers. For example, one Saturday, an older, former tobacco grower who had sold produce on the side saw my stand buzzing with customers. He stopped by after the flurry to ask simply, "What is that?" pointing to a few remaining bags of the greens that seemed to fly off the table an hour earlier. "That's arugula, Howard," I replied. "It's easy to grow and people love it here in Chapel Hill." The next season he was selling arugula, too, and then eventually transitioned out of tobacco altogether, as all of us benefited from the diversity and improvement in our offerings.

But all was not so sanguine across the state. Though our Chapel Hill market was thriving, tens of thousands of farmers like those I had worked with in the UFO were still struggling to pay their bills. Our success with local marketing was having no effect in the far reaches of the state. For every Howard shifting to an upscale farmers market, there were two hundred other farmers flailing in debt or contract growing, with no credit, and fighting racism in isolated rural places. For these traditional family farms, agriculture was still a losing proposition. Though I was succeeding with my alternative plan, I knew that the moratorium on foreclosures was only temporary, and in the not-too-distant future, farm loans would come due and too many would have no way to repay their debts, eventually succumbing to economic pressures.

It was also troubling that our new approach to growing and marketing had done little to improve the diets of poor people. One reason was because our market had gained a reputation for being expensive. And it was also true that social spaces can be surrounded by invisible borders that people who feel they don't belong will not cross. I loved the customers we had—especially because so many of them were already well educated in food issues—but our market had become a food boutique of sorts, mostly for the prosperous.

Those were the big reasons why I welcomed the opportunity to work with Social Services when they approached me, as market president, with a plan to encourage young mothers to use WIC vouchers to buy from our growers. After our board of directors agreed to adopt the plan, young women started showing up the very next week accompanied by caseworkers. The plan was to have them purchase our produce using vouchers that we growers could exchange for cash at the end of the day. When several of the young mothers approached my stand, I was eager to pile collards or kale into bags at the slightest hint that they were interested in cooking, always charging a lower price than my signs said. This gave me a good feeling, but the exchanges also highlighted the disparities in the food system both locally and in society at large. What our effort really proved was that if people know about, and have access to, food alternatives, they will try them. As I already knew from previous experiences, changes in food production and distribution can lead to better diets, and better diets do lead to better health. But we didn't need new data to know that poor people generally can't afford to buy healthy and local. It was already obvious that obesity and other forms of malnourishment existed right in the shadows of our food mecca, and a main cause was food policies that favored profits over people.

Inequality in the food system was not our market's fault, of course, but it wore on me that even as we succeeded at educating our clientele about supporting local growers and buying in season, the agricultural establishment continued pursuing an industrial food agenda, spending millions on research and development leading to corporatized global food trade and ultimately to producing cheaper food that is bad for people and the environment. Junk food marketing, as much as poverty, had helped create our widespread malnourishment in the richest country in the world. Though niche marketing had thrived in enclaves like ours, agribusiness was still raking in billions on food of questionable value. On top of that, segregated communities meant that some neighborhoods simply had better food outlets. Some had no access to produce whatsoever.

Then, as demand increased nationally, large producers began mammoth organic operations in California and started sending their products to destinations near us. Our growers began to realize that not even the word *organic* was ours to control anymore. As far as small growers were concerned, the huge organic farms that shipped food for thousands of miles exacerbated the structural problems we had sought to change in the food system. Though some consumers would soon be able to see organic produce at the chain stores and even at Walmart—which seemed to be a good outcome in some ways—large corporate farms could now compete against small farms in our state. At their gargantuan scale, their sales were never about building communities, but rather were about huge "organic" growers making profits using the same unsavory labor practices as other commercial growers and burning immense quantities of fossil fuels to haul their wares cross-country to capture markets. Their strategy was to build loyalty by way of branding, much like Piggly Wiggly had done back when it became the first self-serve grocery store. The big players used pictures of growers and bucolic scenes of little farms in their advertising, but these idealized images didn't represent farmers that customers would ever meet.

Local farmers like me knew we had been outgunned when the first federal organic farming standards, mandated in 1990, paid no attention to farm size. Soon it was clear that through the argument of standardizing food alternatives, the big food lobbyists had succeeded in taking the words *natural* and *organic* out of the control of the small, local growers. "Big organic," as Michael Pollan later termed it, had been born. As far as we were concerned, the food industry had even usurped our vocabulary. When the USDA began its hearings that decade, we realized that many small growers would not be able to afford the fees to apply for USDA certification as organic growers. Instead of paying to join, some growers decided instead to drop the word *organic* from their signage altogether. We had lost a battle for naming our products in a way that differentiated them from corporate food. No longer was it a contradiction to use *organic* and *corporate* for the same products.

Regardless of terminology, however, I had started to realize that our farms as we organized them individually would never be more than a niche within the ailing world of industrial agriculture. No matter what we farmers grew or what we named it, just down the road, including locales not twenty-five miles from Chapel Hill, contract poultry farming continued to expand exponentially. Wholesale produce markets like those fostered by the state department of agriculture continued as the domain of large growers, and local sellers with limited supplies were shut out of the market by the large grocery chains. At the same time, this fact didn't prevent the big chains from adopting our farmers market terminology. They began to use terms such as *farmer-raised*, *natural*, and even *local* so indiscriminately they became meaningless. One North Carolina grocery chain even slapped a LOCAL sign on any vegetable or fruit produced within a hundred miles of *any* of their hundreds of stores scattered throughout the Southeast. This meant their LOCAL sign could be placed on a product grown a thousand miles away. Then, as a major blow, Whole Foods, out of Austin, Texas, bought out a good locally owned natural foods store I had sold to, eliminating local, small farm relationships with our best store for many of us, and taking away from us primary access even to the so-called natural grocery store world.

The 1980s, in addition to being known as the decade of the American Farm Crisis, became an era of maneuvering for greater dominance by the industrial giants of agriculture. As with poultry, the 1980s and early '90s were when the corporate hog industry consolidated their production with contract agreements with growers who were forced to take all the risk, beginning what came to be called CAFOs (Confined Animal Feeding Operations). As the industry grew, our own North Carolina Senate agriculture chairman, Wendell Murphy, led the NC legislature in 1991 to outlaw any zoning restrictions for contract-style arrangements in any community statewide. This meant that huge hog operations started by swine-farming giant Murphy Farms could move into the rural communities of their choosing, which often meant low-income communities of color, without penalty. Later Murphy would sell his company to Smithfield Foods, but he would retain a strong financial stake in the company, at least until the whole conglomerate sold to WH Group in China in 2013. But this is only the story of one person's rise to power in one commodity. The decade also brought intense lobbying to weaken pesticide regulations and further the consolidation of markets. The Farm Bureau, claiming they represented huge numbers of family farmer members by counting every person who bought insurance from them as a member, also lobbied against drinking water and bathrooms in the fields for farmworkers. Human rights and farmworker advocates were appalled.

Though we had started to see small changes in the North Carolina Agricultural Extension Service—as our county got a new agent versed in organic farming—Hope and her colleagues at RAF, by then called the Rural Advancement Foundation International (RAFI), and later at a Canadian organization called ETC Group, had started to uncover new facts about the promotion of questionable biotechnology and pesticide developments, including at taxpayer-funded land-grant universities. The organizations revealed, among other facts, how agricultural research was feeding the profits of corporations. RAFI was also one of the first advocacy groups to uncover new evidence that agribusiness had started to merge with big pharmaceutical companies, and that seed companies were being gobbled up by agricultural chemical giants. Before long, they showed, that only a handful of major corporations would own and control seed production, agrochemicals, fertilizers, and so would call the shots on research and development in agriculture. Time has proven that their prophecies were on the money.

These were just some of the unsavory realities of big agriculture that I had become keenly aware of as we toiled away at growing and selling produce at our local markets. I started to realize corporate CEOs must have been pleased when "foodies"—people focused intensely on the food on their plates not just for sustenance but as a hobby—put all their efforts into supporting local farmers while taking their eyes off the huge environmental and social impacts of the larger food system. It was as if our nation's farm economy had become bifurcated. On one side, it consisted of a small and idealistic segment that was exchanging products directly between farmers and consumers in trendy towns and cities, and on the other, a vastly more powerful corporate agricultural system that was managing the wholesale domestic and global trading of commodities and controlling every link in the food chain from seed to shelf. Meanwhile, the medium-sized family farmers—including many UFO members— gained nothing in either category and continued to be squeezed out. The small towns that had supported these traditional family farmers were also dying.

Pulling back from my blackberry field long enough to see this bigger picture made me painfully aware that forging agricultural alternatives would never be enough to change the trajectory of our nation's agricultural systems writ large. I began to talk with our customers about agribusiness and about being politically active. These educated consumers, already primed to care about the food system beyond their own dinner tables, wanted to find out how food trade worked, and how to help rectify unfair policies that favored the large over small farms globally. From that starting point, I believed we could endeavor to challenge monopolies in the grain industry, as well as the collusion of pesticide manufacturers with seed distributors, and agribusiness lobbyists with politicians. We could elect progressive commissioners of agriculture on the state level and organize to elect leaders who would do the same on the federal level and at the USDA. I dreamed that if those people who frequented local farmers markets could use their influence to champion sustainable agriculture, not just locally, but nationally and globally, for all farmers, then we could bring about the change we sought.

I had discovered that despite the appearance of bifurcation, there really aren't two different food systems: an alternative one for those who are "enlightened" and lucky enough to live near markets, and another that provides for everyone else. The reality is that while some of us live in the right locations, are well educated about what to eat, can access good food, and possess enough affluence to maneuver through the food world, no one ever truly escapes industrial agriculture. I was reminded of this point by the very air I breathed on Whippoorwill Farm. When on some rare days the wind blew from the northeast, I could smell the Webster's Poultry processing plant—located only two miles away—while I worked. Though I had been outside planting and harvesting in a pesticide-free field and breathing in the earthy smell of compost, this intrusive smell of factory-farm offal and death reminded me there were people inside a windowless plant, standing in ice and blood, eviscerating birds all day long, and breathing all that filth into their lungs. I could not block the wind from leaving that tainted factory environment and drifting into my nostrils, either. Go anywhere, and the industrial food system will still blow its filth toward you from not so far away. Hence, food politics can never be just about "what's for dinner," but must also be about the food everyone else is eating.

Chicken catcher, Chatham County, 1987. Photograph by Rob Amberg.

Processing | *1986*

One hot June afternoon, five men drove into our driveway in a beat-up Impala, stepped out, and with a handshake, fused Whippoorwill Farm into the international immigration system. That week our farm's blackberry plants and vegetables had exploded beyond my capacity to harvest them all. Until that week, the few local teenagers who helped me part-time had been sufficient. Though they worked hard, their commitment had begun to wane as the summer grew hotter and new job opportunities—including working in the nearby Hardee's fast-food restaurant—came along. With no one scheduled to help on Monday and several deliveries promised to grocery stores and restaurants, and a Tuesday farmers market coming up, I asked my neighbor Kenny if he had any ideas on finding help for harvest. He advised me to go to the local chicken plant to ask his friend Joe, a foreman over the evisceration line, to help put out the word. Kenny said, "He told me those Mexicans they brought in to work at the plant are ready to make money and would probably help you. You just need to let him know."

I met Joe at the plant during his break on Monday morning and explained that I needed blackberry and vegetable pickers that afternoon and gave him directions to our place. He agreed to put out the word, adding that he would ask a bilingual worker to help him talk to others in the plant. Not knowing whether such a plan could work, I started harvesting on my own that afternoon. I filled my garden cart with dozens of berry flats and loose cartons, and I pushed it toward the field. Looking at the long rows ahead of me, I had begun to despair a little when Librado, Eusebio, Faustino, Juan, and Luis drove in. They spoke softly to one another as they got out

175

of their old car, assessing the situation. Standing in the driveway in their bloodied white lab coats and black rubber boots, breathing in the open air of the farm, they waited for me to approach. I introduced myself as best I knew how, shaking their hands and saying, "*Bienvenidos.*"

Faustino was both the youngest member of the group and the most fluent in English. He asked if I needed them to "pick *frutas?*" I replied, "*Sí, gracias!*" Then I pointed to the field and explained with hand motions and by picking up the empty flats that we still needed some forty of these twelve-pint holders filled with only the ripest blackberries. "*Moras*" is what they are called in Spanish, they said. They needed no further orientation to method, as Faustino asked simply, "Where?" When I showed them the rows, he asked, "How much do you pay?" When I offered them an hourly wage I knew was higher than they were making in the chicken plant, they proposed instead to pick by the flat. When I agreed on the price they stated, they set off running through the fields, harvesting nearly as fast as I could carry the flats to the cooler. I learned later they had already worked in strawberry and tomato fields in Florida before coming to North Carolina. They knew more about harvesting produce than I did. Their goal was to maximize their time, and to make as much money as possible by the hour and still get home to make their supper before bed. They finished the blackberries in one-tenth the time it would have taken me alone, and then started on harvesting the vegetables. I was elated to realize that we were going to finish before dark.

I have since seen a photograph of a billboard that a North Carolina–based poultry company put up in Oaxaca, Mexico. The big poultry processing plants had started advertising for workers almost as soon as the concrete was being poured for the poultry processing plant floors in rural North Carolina. Enticing rural immigrants to do indoor work in the United States was part of their unwritten business plan. By the mid-1980s, as the poultry industry was taking off, Latino men, many of them young and traveling without families at first, began arriving in our county by the hundreds. They would work as chicken catchers and processing line workers—the worst poultry jobs—instantly making themselves indispensable to the surging industry. Forced to keep up with the speed of whizzing machines, few locals wanted the jobs for the paltry wages the plants were offering. But those newly arrived from the border, whose wages back home were one-tenth of the US minimum, desperately needed the jobs, even if they hated the smelly conditions, the freezing temperatures, and performing the same repetitive motion for hours on end. As new immigrants without papers, they had no alternative work, and thus were confined to agricultural jobs, even as agriculture mechanized and businesses concentrated into fewer hands.

As the factories began using their new contract system on farms—which places most of the risk of owning land, building barns, and raising the birds on the farmers, as FmHA had encouraged—and employing low-wage laborers in the plants, chicken prices dipped. Every day, truckloads of boxed chicken parts were shipped from Pittsboro to locations all over the Southeast. Meanwhile, contract growers were sending birds to the plant by the hundreds of thousands every day. Novelist Doris Betts compared the feather cover along the roadsides in our community to year-round snow. She was right, but snow was the furthest thing from my mind on that hot afternoon in June 1986 when the globalizing agricultural system brought men across borders to our local organic farm. As there had been no other way for me to harvest my fruit, how grateful I was that the border had crossed my farm and now new immigrants had changed my entire agricultural outlook for the future.

The men came back two or three days a week for the rest of the berry season, and with Hope's help I began to speak to them in broken Spanish. Hope had become fluent in Spanish as a child in Texas, and when she got home from her job, she helped me communicate with them. I also began studying Spanish, taking a pocket dictionary with me to the field. Between Faustino's rudimentary English and my beginning efforts at Spanish, we started to share stories. The five men had come from the state of Nayarit, where many farmers grew tobacco. Faustino was Eusebio's son. Both had left their wives and children behind. The other three were either cousins or friends from the same community. The fact that hit me hardest was that they were all farmers back in Nayarit. When their dwindling farm income failed to cover their bills, they were forced to migrate, traveling thousands of miles to help their families—and now others who hired them—have a better life.

Theirs was not unlike the story of my own family, just in a different era. Mine were immigrant ancestors from Europe who had sought a toehold in the steep hollows of Appalachia. Now I was hearing echoes of my family's journey in Spanish. Their trip was hard and dangerous, they said. None wanted to leave their families, but this was their only option. Their parents or children remained behind awaiting their remittances, and the men wired money and phoned them almost weekly. Selling phone cards and making money transfers over thousands of miles to Latin America was a new business in our county, allowing family members in Mexico to benefit almost immediately from money earned in the United States. Thus, in the process of saving my harvest, they were helping save their land as well. We had entered into an international interdependency, albeit an unequal one. No matter how much I tried to befriend the men—and I did try hard—it was clear to all of us that our relationship was one-sided, especially in terms of the privileges of ownership and citizenship. That difference was apparent from their first arrival and was a fact I had no power to change.

I knew something about how the immigration system worked from prior experiences. While at Jubilee Partners in Georgia, Hope had worked with Central American refugees who were seeking asylum in Canada. I had also been on the periphery of an organization that she had volunteered with as they helped two different refugees come to Pittsboro. One of them had stayed for a while in our house. My own present involvement in immigration had less to do with humanitarianism; this was my livelihood. Whether I liked it or not, I had become another North Carolina farmer newly dependent on "foreign labor."

I struggled with how this new reality meshed with my vision for social change. I had no interest in exploiting people for my gain, but

I knew I couldn't pretend I was somehow free of the contradictions of farming, either. I decided to address the realities of international farm losses and agricultural injustices head-on, as I put faces and names with the story of how big conglomerates, some of them growing fat on agricultural subsidies from the US government, were squeezing small farmers out of Mexico, too. I had read about how US-subsidized food exports were dumping low-priced commodities and displacing tens of thousands of smaller growers all over the world. But now I knew five of the displaced by name. The depersonalized story of global trade and economics paled in comparison with the farmworkers' stories of their families back home and the smiling faces of children in the wrinkled photographs they showed me. These stories made me aware of my own standing in global agriculture. I was a young farmer trying to buy his own small farm (though independent of any company and beholden to no one except the FmHA), now hiring immigrant laborers with proceeds from my *local* sales in Chapel Hill. I knew these five farmworkers were only present in my community because of immigration associated with corporate agriculture, but now I was also benefiting from their labor as I sold to the alternative markets I had helped develop. The multiple ironies were not lost on me, including the fact that my "local" crops would be harvested by global labor.

My Spanish improved, and I began learning more about the workers' lives, both on the chicken processing line and beyond. But I never got comfortable with the role I played. I tried breaking down the border between us, asking the men to teach me about Mexico and the migrant system of labor they were part of, even as I tried to show them a different side of the United States. But there was no getting around the fact that they were laborers of color with few rights in our country, and that I benefited from the inequities that existed at the international scale that had pushed them to Pittsboro. Regardless of my attitude, Mexico remained a developing country adjacent to the richest one in the world, and that disparity was the reason why I could hire the men. I earned money from their work because of international exchange and inequalities that stretched back centuries to the beginning of our nation's exploitation of Mexico's land and people. Regardless of how much I paid the five men, they were working in a foreign land they could own no part of, while I was buying a farm with the proceeds they helped me earn. This was not at all the model of agriculture I had dreamed of creating! Instead of building a new economic model, I felt I was now a reluctant party to a system of labor exchange that had presented a moral quandary on American farms dating back to American farming's most famous apologist, Thomas Jefferson. I agonized over how to do something to change this.

During the first year the five men worked for me, Faustino asked me to sign papers to help them qualify for green cards under the provisions of the Immigration Reform and Control Act of 1986, and I readily agreed that I would. In spirit at least, I had already become their ally, and I was happy to help them in some tangible way. But more important, they had begun to teach me that my prime interest in farming was not personal landownership or being successful as an organic grower after all, but rather learning and showing how and why so many people who had worked America's soil, harvested its produce, and butchered its animals had been treated like dirt. These five men had come thousands of miles just to hold on to farms back home, and in doing so, they showed me again why my deepest devotion had always been to the people of farming, and that human stories of agriculture were my first love.

Charlie Thompson, *seated*, with farmers in Iredell County, North Carolina feed mill in 1986. Photograph by Rob Amberg.

Selling | *1993*

*W*ith the help of Faustino and Librado on Saturday afternoons and Sundays, I built oak board fences around the house and barn and painted them white. When we finished, they looked nearly like the fences at my grandparents' farm. We painted the barn red just like theirs, too. The fences were freshly painted when I decided to buy and breed three of my grandfather's Hereford heifers to start my own herd from his. Grandpa, now too old to drive, had ridden down to North Carolina with my father in the same big truck we had taken to the Hollins Livestock Market. I was elated that he and his truck were still going strong, and that Grandpa could see our farm coming into its own.

I had anticipated that the delivery of the cattle would be a powerful symbol of interfamilial exchange and a way for me to receive Grandpa's legacy. I wanted my family to be proud, and I had hoped that by mimicking some of my favorite parts of Grandpa's farm I would rekindle the feelings we shared when I was living and working with him. Instead, these symbols only made our farm seem sad to me. When Grandpa left with Dad and headed back to Ferrum after unloading the cattle, I felt so alone, freshly aware of the gaping hole at Whippoorwill Farm that in a perfect world would have been filled by extended family. I went into the house and said to Hope, "No matter how hard I work, I will never re-create Grandpa's farm here. No matter what, I'll always feel that something is missing." The words emerged from deep within me. They meant that all the labor I'd put into the farm had failed to provide me the grounding I sought. My labor had not been in vain, as I had turned a farm into something to be proud of, but I knew that what I had been seeking was still elusive.

I had gotten to know the last traditional family farmers remaining in our community, including the newcomers, the Clouses. But now that John had lost his poultry contract, he had gone to work for a golf course and was no longer around during the day. Mary, much to our delight, had gone to work for the Rural Advancement Fund as a poultry farmer advocate. Two other farmers, whom we called affectionately Mr. Lacey and Mr. Bill, were well over eighty years old. They were holdovers from the community's agricultural past. Neither worked full-time anymore. These farmers became special neighbors, but our daily lives were of different worlds. Though I got truckloads of old chicken manure from the Clouses for my fields, and Mr. Lacey and Mr. Bill helped me with my hay for our small sheep flock, no one around me worked in their fields by day. With Hope working in an office in town, I was the only farmer around during most days, at least until the men arrived from the chicken plant a few days a week.

When our son Marshall was born, he added immeasurable depth to our lives and meaning to my farming experience. I cared for him on many afternoons, often in the fields. More than once he rode with me, in a backpack and under an umbrella, as I drove the tractor tiller through the vegetable beds. But he, too, needed an extended family to make a farm really work. Hope and I talked longingly of make-believe cousins and uncles and grandparents living nearby, knowing we were a little nuclear family alone and in need of a farming village. Good friends of ours helped raise Marshall, but few were interested in helping raise crops. My farmers market friends were one community we were part of, but during the week we were dispersed within a fifty-mile radius from Carrboro.

Cultivating or harvesting in the fields by myself gave me time to ponder the stories that lay within the soil beneath me. I imagined those who had worked the fields in the past. A few of the descendants of the Fawcett family who had last raised tobacco and cotton on the farm stopped by to introduce themselves. They were the last to farm our place for a living before us, and extended family members still lived close by, though all of them had left agriculture by the time we came along. A few times Wayne Fawcett, one of the grandsons, drove up, got out of his car, and leaned against it in our driveway to talk with me. He seemed grateful to know someone cared for the place. But it was obvious he had no desire to return to the work. He remembered from his youth having to hoe out seemingly endless rows of tobacco and carrying nicotine-ridden leaves under his arm as he harvested them. He must have thought only a madman would work so hard by himself, but I'm sure the main reason he stopped by was because part of him still remained there in that soil.

Because I was always asking about the history of the place we lived on, I learned one day that the Fawcetts were not the first named family who had worked our land. A neighbor had recommended that I talk with an elderly, retired, African American sharecropper named Mr. Oldham, adding that he was one of our community's eldest inhabitants, and he might remember something about the history of our farm. Mr. Oldham lived with his wife and adult daughter along the highway a mile or so from our farm. I knocked on their door one afternoon, told them where I lived, and shared a few details about myself. Mr. Oldham's daughter invited me into the house and offered me a seat in the living room across from her father. He was sitting on a sofa, his metal walker beside him. I shook his hand, sat down, and got right to my questions about the place. He was ready to tell what he knew. What he told me was staggering.

"When I was a child, there was a family of Black farmers on that place," he said. He remembered the family's last name was Peoples. "They raised cotton on the land," he said, "and they farmed with mules." He did not know how they had come by the land to begin with, but he said they had put the farm up as collateral to purchase a team of mules. "Then they had a bad crop year and they lost them mules and then they come in and took the house and the whole farm, too," he said. "They," of course, were white people. There was a tone of resignation in his voice. How many times had that same story of loss been repeated among Black farmers? How many farm families had Mr. Oldham seen leave their land in his lifetime? I knew of only one remaining African American farmer in our entire county. Now I had learned that no matter how hard I had tried to reverse Black land loss in my work, it was part of the history of the place I owned. I did not know how to apologize to a family now gone, but I wanted somehow to ask forgiveness of Mr. Oldham for all of America's sordid history. He might have wondered why I said "I'm sorry" to him as I thanked the family and bid them good-bye.

From that day on, every time I dug into the soil, I thought of those now invisible people who had worked the same land before me. As I did so, I came to realize that anyone's possession of land almost always means another's loss. Of course, there are amicable transfers of land, but I'm referring to land loss in which one party is forced to leave or sell, and there are many strata of such histories in the United States. And now that I had learned that Whippoorwill Farm also had such a story, I had to acknowledge that my farming was due to earlier forfeitures and losses by people I would never meet.

As I turned up old mule shoes or plow points in the soil, I saved them as a tribute to the Peoples. When I clutched fistfuls of soil and closed my eyes, I could almost hear their voices. Though I found no further facts about the Peoples, they came alive to me through signs. Their universal-sounding name also stuck with me, and it came to mean everyman and everywoman who had once loved land anywhere and lost it. The Peoples became all of the farmers who had labored but had no land to show for it. They are legion.

At some point in time, the Peoples found a piece of America they could call their own. Perhaps it was during Reconstruction, which was enforced by the US government soldiers following the Civil War. But as the soldiers left and headed back North after Rutherford B. Hayes's election, race hatred and resentment boiled over in their wake. The KKK, Jim Crow, and vagrancy laws all arose as backlashes to Black landownership and independence, effectively seeking to maintain Black subservience and poverty for generations. Black landowners, in particular, became targets of vigilante groups like the Klan, though the bankers' loan policies were often just as effective at getting rid of African American farmers, which was one reason the Rural Resettlement Administration had been created. In the case of the Peoples's farm, a team of mules was all it took to put the land back into white hands. And now we had inherited and lived with this story. No amount of sustainable farming language could obscure the fact that I was working land where a silent racial cleansing had taken place.

While I farmed in the 1980s, African American farmers continued to lose their land at an unprecedented rate. Even after winning a class action lawsuit against the USDA, proving widespread discrimination based on race, African American farmers waited for decades to receive their due. Would there ever be a new generation of Black farmers to enter US agriculture to replace those who had gone? Given my experience with farm lending, I was almost sure that had I been Black, no FmHA office would have touched my loan.

In the same farm soil, I also found projectile points. They were, as Thoreau had said of his bean field discoveries in *Walden*, remnants of "unchronicled nations who in primeval years lived under these heavens." These points, which I kept in my top dresser drawer, were tangible proof that our same land had been used by indigenous peoples thousands of years earlier for farming and hunting. As with the mule shoes, my thoughts about farming changed dramatically as I picked up the stone objects and held them, with the past coming to life in my present. Though, as far as I knew, I was unrelated to anyone who had ever worked our farm, I now felt a kinship with them through the soil we had shared.

★ ★ ★

Some seven years into my time at Whippoorwill Farm, I began to rethink the very meaning of farming. Some revelations came from the soil beneath me, and from people speaking from beyond recorded history. Lessons about land tenure that had formed in my childhood had only deepened in the places I had traveled and among the people with whom I had worked. All of this experiential education led to the single, large discovery that the American Dream of farming was in fact a myth. From there, I realized that I needed to read and perhaps take classes to work this out and to share what I had learned. I started to feel compelled to articulate what I was finding through writing, and perhaps through filmmaking as well. But how should I proceed? Where should I go to school, and by what means might I get there?

One afternoon when I was trying to keep busy in the farmhouse while Marshall was down for his nap, I decided to make one last attempt to settle the old promise I had made to Grandpa. Before exploring a new path to tell farmers' stories on page and screen, I needed to know if the vet school option might work for me. I called up the admissions office at the vet school at North Carolina State University to talk with them about enrolling. The admissions officer asked about my academic background; despite my arts and humanities and agricultural education tracks, she still encouraged me to apply. There would be some remedial work to do, she explained in a confident voice, "So you will need to take undergraduate courses at a community college. You'll need to take organic chemistry, biology, anatomy courses, and more, but after you do well on those, you'll have a very good chance of getting in." My heart sank. Vet school had been a nagging source of guilt for decades since I'd promised Grandpa I would go. But now I knew that I had no interest in any of the courses the admissions rep mentioned. Plus, Grandpa would never have wanted me to pursue a career that didn't inspire me. By the time the school's shiny brochures depicting smiling young people working happily with cattle, horses, and dogs arrived in the mail, I had already made up my mind that a career doctoring animals was not for me, even though it would allow me to work with farmers.

Then on a spring weekend, a group of students from East Carolina University spent two days working with us on our farm. My most meaningful exchange with them came not from the work we did together, but when I spoke with them about my farming philosophy, which now included the hidden histories I had uncovered. I had prepared a Wendell Berry poem as a reading, and included the mule shoes and arrowheads as teaching tools. Later that summer, I agreed to do a feasibility study for a teaching farm at an Episcopal conference center in Valle Crucis, North Carolina. When I began writing up my ideas, a dam broke and over eighty pages of prose about farms, history, and culture gushed out. Experiences like those began to suggest over time that a university PhD program could possibly be for me.

In my eighth year of farming, I began to talk with professors who were my customers at the Carrboro Farmers' Market about applying to graduate school at the University of North Carolina. A well-known English professor named Robert Kirkpatrick, who loved eating our lamb and regularly came to buy it, said, "You don't want to go to graduate school just to put out one more academic book into the world." But upon seeing how different my motivations were from that, he found a tutor to help me prepare for the GRE entrance exams. His colleague and my neighbor, Doris Betts, promised to write a recommendation letter. She gave me confidence when she said, "You write, so you're a writer." I started telling friends I was thinking about grad school. My bubble burst when a religious studies professor, also a market customer, told me point blank that I should leave my farm and organizing experiences out of my application. "First of all, you should omit any mention of your farming," he said. "Instead, your letter needs to be entirely academic." I was dumbfounded at first. But his advice turned out to be the impetus I needed, only in reverse.

That fall I decided to apply to the UNC program called Religion and Culture, a hybrid of religious studies and cultural anthropology, a field of study that combines philosophy and ethnographic fieldwork. In my letter to the department, I put my experiences as a farmer and organizer front and center. Those experiences, I wrote, prompted the central questions I wanted to explore. If I had to fake who I was to get in, I didn't want to be part of their department anyway. As it turned out, farming *was* my ticket in. Years after I had completed the program, I found out from Martha Tyson, the wife of my advisor, Professor Ruel Tyson, that upon receiving my application, he exclaimed to her, "We had a farmer apply today!"

My peculiarity made me stand out, where my academic background alone would have put me at the back of the pack.

When I first began the program, I was naive enough to think I could farm and study at the same time. Then, after completing the fall semester, in the midst of a heated argument with Hope at the end of December, it became obvious that it would be impossible for me to continue carrying the load of family, farm, and graduate school simultaneously. I knew my temper had risen from overwork. We had to sell the farm. So during winter break I called a realtor friend in Chapel Hill and we listed the place. The first week the farm went on the market, we received five offers higher than the asking price. Clearly by 1993, the idea of organic farming had started taking root in North Carolina. Nine years after my FmHA loan had gone through, Librado, Faustino, and I had improved the soil and appearance of one worn-out tobacco farm to such an extent that now people were clamoring to buy it. A working organic farm complete with painted fences and outbuildings, berry plants, apple trees, and well-manured vegetable beds was enticing even to those who had no farm experience, or frighteningly, to those who had never even gardened.

My focus in graduate school would be on borders, the politics of places, and the meaning of indigeneity in light of global migration, of being native to bleeding land. Part of my motivation was my own story, specifically my efforts to re-create a sense of home. I had pulled up my own shallow roots in order to study refugees, immigrants, and migrant workers—all of them also searching for home and stability. These focuses were the direct result of my digging in the ground where I had found not so much a strong sense of my own rootedness, but rather the layered losses of others displaced. Though I had never been a refugee or a migrant searching for work, I still identified as a sojourner. While digging into and adding fertility to a plot of ground is one of the best ways to engender a sense of belonging to it, I then realized how fragile any sense of place really is. Being from somewhere and belonging to it is not a commodity that can be purchased or even an idea that one can create single-handedly.

Rather, a strong sense of home grows from ancestral work and family memories, sacrifices, cultures, rituals, histories, and, most important, stories passed down over generations that are told again and again. Being part of a story of land, in other words, requires the active work of clinging to histories through generations. When there is an injustice present in soil, the work of belonging includes conducting an archaeology of habitation in that place, an excavation of injustices that must be addressed in the present.

Though I had added tons of humus and quarts of my own sweat to one piece of land, I had not found a true home in it. Maybe part of the reason was because people had not done enough to address the injustices that lay beneath Whippoorwill Farm, or for that matter, any part of the Americas and beyond. My digging into soil had only unearthed more questions. Unable to ignore the tens of millions moved off their farms against their will past and present, I wanted to devote myself to further listening to the stories of the displaced. Beginning to write and make films, I sought to amplify the voices of rural people, and help share their stories, particularly those who had once loved places and were forced to leave them. I would listen for the voices of the unsettled, the landless, and the stymied would-be farmers who were still seeking home places in an unjust world. My quest was in part autobiographical, as so many studies are, but I knew that my search was much broader and deeper than one person's story. My quest was to know the stories of America's lost people and places, knowing I would have to cross borders to find them.

Pancho Ros, Maya coffee farmer in Jacaltenango, Guatemala.

Reaping | *1997*

O ne of the stories I heard while still on Whippoorwill Farm that most influenced my decision to go back to school belonged to a Guatemalan man named Victor Montejo. Victor was one of the refugees helped by the volunteer Carolina Interfaith Taskforce on Central America (CITCA) organization that Hope had joined in Pittsboro. Victor's journey to North Carolina began when his brother Pedro was murdered by a death squad in the middle of the town square of Jacaltenango, his hometown, as he celebrated his graduation from teacher's training. The offense was merely being loud while drinking. At the time, teachers and other leaders in indigenous communities like his were targets of Rios Montt's ruling junta because they were suspected of becoming agitators. Following Pedro Montejo's death, Victor himself was tortured and would have been killed had he not found a way to flee to Mexico. In his wallet he carried the phone number of a friend of ours named Wallace who had given the number to Pedro while the two were riding a bus. Pedro kept the number because in their conversation Wallace revealed that he is a writer, and Pedro wanted Victor, also a writer, and Wallace to get together. Pedro passed along the number to Victor, which he kept, but never called, until he got to Mexico. Having fled for his life in the dark a few nights before, Victor phoned Wallace in Pittsboro to ask for safe harbor. Wallace, remembering Pedro, agreed. Victor's life (and those of many people he would come in contact with) would never be the same.

After Victor arrived in Pittsboro, Wallace got in touch with the local CITCA chapter. This small cohort of like-minded friends helped sponsor Victor. As a result, he moved in with friends of ours in Pittsboro for an entire year. I joined in the effort, mostly by giving

Victor driving lessons and teaching him a little English in my spare time. Despite my peripheral involvement in CITCA, I was deeply moved by Victor's story of violence and flight from his homeland.

When we last saw Victor in the mid-1980s, the former grade school teacher was headed to Canada, where he would receive asylum and reunite with his extended family. After he left, only bits of news filtered back to us about Victor. One incredible fact we learned was that Victor had continued to study and write, and he had earned his PhD in anthropology at the University of Connecticut. Years later we learned that he had landed a professorship in the Department of Native American Studies at the University of California, Davis. We were awestruck.

I reconnected with Dr. Victor Montejo thirteen years after his arrival in Pittsboro when I was in graduate school, this time at a national anthropology meeting in Atlanta. After searching in vain for him for several hours after my arrival at the conference, I finally found Victor when I entered the large meeting hall for a plenary session. Much to my surprise, he was sitting on stage next to Coretta Scott King. After Mrs. King's welcome to Atlanta and other opening remarks, Victor stood at the lectern and gave a talk on indigenous rights, in perfect English.

Immediately after the session ended, I rushed through the crowd to the stage to reintroduce myself. Luckily, he remembered me. I told him right away about my return to school. Then I told him in a few sentences how his arrival had influenced my desire to study in Guatemala. He suggested we meet for lunch the next day at a small café in the conference hotel. There, Victor not only approved of my doing fieldwork in Guatemala—a symbolic endorsement I had sought—but also invited my family to live in his house in Jacaltenango, and said that he would help me study in the nearby satellite village where his parents had returned from Canada to live. The year was 1997, when UN peace accords ended a thirty-year civil war and the country was patrolled by an international peacekeeping force. I couldn't wait to return to Chapel Hill to inform my dissertation committee. After they approved the new focus, I went to visit Victor and his family in

Jacaltenango for a few days over spring break, and returned knowing that Jacalteco refugees would be the focus of my fieldwork. I rewrote my dissertation proposal based on Victor's invitation and background help. When that also received hearty approval by my committee, we decided to take Victor up on his offer to rent his house. A few months later, Hope, Marshall—then seven years old—and I drove in our pickup truck from North Carolina to Guatemala, tracing in reverse the miles that so many Central American refugees traveled to the United States. After arriving in Jacaltenango, known as the *cabecera*, or head town, of the wider area, I began conducting my fieldwork in La Laguna, a smaller hamlet an hour away. Everyone living in La Laguna had until recently been refugees, having fled one night after being attacked by a death squad.

During the time I lived there, many Jacaltecos continued to arrive back from exile each week. By then, a majority had been out of the country for thirteen years. Through their stories of living in Mexico, the United States, and Canada, these Jacalteco Maya taught me that there is no passive means of being indigenous to a place. Their indigeneity, especially in absentia, required constant reinvention and rebuilding. And even back in their home in La Laguna, their work of identity maintenance continued. They taught me just how hard it is to be indigenous in a place so long contested.

I returned to the United States profoundly changed by having lived among farmers who had maintained their connections to their land despite more than a decade of forced exile. The more I studied Maya history and talked with those who had been refugees, the more the Maya showed me that this struggle to maintain their dignity as indigenous people had been the norm for them for centuries. They had endured over five hundred years of colonialism, managing, against all odds, to live as Maya despite racism and enslavement. The Jacaltecos taught me that being indigenous to a place is not so much about genetics or blood, but about the hard work of maintaining one's sense of belonging amid constant trials and challenges.

Upon my return, my experiences in Guatemala inspired me to pursue two new focuses. The first was my turn to farmworker advocacy, work of the heart that I have since maintained for over twenty years. I had learned firsthand from Librado, Eusebio, Faustino, Juan, and Luis on my own farm about what it means for migrants to leave family behind, but in Jacaltenango I saw up close how much is lost in such a transition. One Jacalteco friend described going to the United States as splitting his heart in two, leaving one piece behind and taking one with him. I learned that such departures are rarely chosen but are often thrust on people by both violence and economic inequality. For so many, leaving requires sacrificing one's own needs and desires for the sake of others. Very few leave an indigenous community without ripping themselves apart.

Getting back to North Carolina with this new knowledge, I immediately contacted Melinda Wiggins, director of Student Action with Farmworkers, to let her know I wanted to help the cause. Soon I was on the board of directors. Later, Melinda and I began editing the book *The Human Cost of Food: Farmworkers' Lives, Labor, and Advocacy*, in which I wrote a chapter about Whippoorwill Farm that I titled "Layers of Loss." The chapter concludes with the following:

> We as a nation have become dependent upon displaced farmers from elsewhere to do our hand labor in the fields. We eat because of their losses. U.S. agriculture depends on the displaced. Indeed, it always has.*

A second new focus was to try to understand my family's agricultural heritage in the context of European exile, this time concentrating on my mother's side. Prior to leaving for Guatemala, I had conducted a semester of fieldwork among the Old German Baptist Brethren for

---

* Charles D. Thompson, Jr. and Melinda Wiggins, *Human Cost of Food: Farmworkers' Lives, Labor, and Advocacy* (Austin: University of Texas Press, 2002), 86.

my master's thesis. After completing *The Human Cost of Food* and publishing my dissertation, "Maya Identities and the Violence of Place," I picked up where I left off on the story of German immigrants in the 1700s. These were my grandmother Jamison's people.

From childhood, I had known Grandma Jamison was the daughter and granddaughter of ministers in the Brethren church. I had seen pictures of her as a young woman when she had worn a bonnet and long dress to mark her membership in the group that some refer to as the Old Order. Her maiden name was Ikenberry, an anglicized version of Eichenberg. Her ancestors were among some of the earliest European farmers to arrive in Franklin County. They, too, had been exiles, many working as indentured servants before migrating to the Blue Ridge in search of farms.

Through this research, I found that during the time of the Virginia frontier settlements, Thomas Jefferson, though he owned African slaves, occasionally mused about how to change agriculture from the system of chattel slavery to one that relied instead on European renters or sharecroppers. Knowing how human enslavement belied our nation's emphasis on freedom, he fantasized about replacing enslaved people with tenants. He wrote a number of letters to friends and relatives recommending that the best candidates to employ on American plantations for a tenant system could be Germans from the Palatinate or Rhine region. He wrote while in Paris to Thomas Claiborne, for example, "Of all foreigners I should prefer Germans. They are the easiest got, the best for their landlord, and do best for themselves."[*]

In conversations with several historians at Monticello, including Dr. Cinder Stanton and Dr. Christa Dierksheide, I ascertained that Jefferson may even have had German small farmers of the Shenandoah Valley in mind when he wrote the famous line, "Cultivators of the earth are the

---

[*] Thomas Jefferson, *The Papers of Thomas Jefferson, Volume 12: 7 August 1787 to 31 March 1788*, ed. Julian P. Boyd (Princeton, NJ: Princeton University Press, 1955).

most virtuous and independant [*sic*] citizens."* He had certainly passed by their farms on his governmental trips to Pennsylvania, the historians explained, and thus the influences for that writing could have been German immigrants. We are already aware of the irony of the author of the Declaration of Independence owning slaves. But herein could exist a second major contradiction in his thinking about citizenship. Specifically, his suggestion that planters might use German farmers as *métayers*, a French term referring to a type of sharecropper, would seem to contradict his idea of independent farmer-citizens who could champion liberty. Instead, Jefferson's musings on citizenship appear clouded by his suggestion of using un-landed people to help them work their farms. Does this mean the central irony of the American agricultural story originates not only with enslaved peoples, but also with the notion that foreigners could work in their stead as a non-landowning class? Yes, I am convinced that Jefferson, in conversation with other agrarians, lauded a democratic form of farm ownership while owning slaves and recommending sharecropping by Germans as slavery's alternative. We know many of these exemplary German farmers had to work years for wealthy landowners before they gained the independence Jefferson touted. These cultivators were not the chosen of God by birthright, in other words, but were workers using their sweat to pay off their debts.

And why were many indebted to begin with? Most German immigrants from the Palatinate region, like my ancestors, were exiles in flight from religious persecution following the Thirty Years' War. Jefferson didn't indicate in his letters that he knew most Palatinate Germans were, in fact, seeking peace and the freedom to practice their faith. He didn't discuss that when the Germans finally found land on which to practice their religious beliefs, it was their exile—along with emphasis on community, religion, and family—that likely made them the diligent farmers he observed. Jefferson did say in a letter to American Federal Commissioners, however, while still

---

* Thomas Jefferson, *Notes on the State of Virginia* (New York: Penguin Books, 1999), 181.

speaking about their promise as tenants: "They are distinguished for their industry and sobriety, and might do good as an example and model to be referred to."* The resonances between what Jefferson said about my German Palatinate immigrant ancestors and what farmers say about today's Mexican farmworkers are haunting.

It makes logical sense that regardless of country of origin, few immigrants to America from three centuries ago or now ever left their homes, went into debt, sailed across the Atlantic or crossed borders or any other obstacle hoping merely to work for others and remain humble renters or laborers. Even in the 1700s, speculators knew that people desired land, and they worked to capitalize on this. Labor contractors sought out German immigrants in Amsterdam and other ports, and they passed out flyers touting the false claim of the great abundance of American land that was free for the taking and so encouraging emigration. Contradicting the promises made on these flyers was that most indentured people who worked on farms arrived in debt and had to work four to seven years before they could start farming on their own.† As many as two-thirds of new immigrants were forced into indentured servitude, and thereby sacrificed some of their most productive years to benefit others. During their time of indenture, the "sober industriousness" of these nonlandowner farmworkers went not toward building the democratic participatory ownership system Jefferson championed on paper, but toward enriching the coffers of landlords who had come by their places through grants, inheritance, and old wealth—like the plantations held by Jefferson's family.

But the story doesn't end there. The desire for landownership cannot be worked out of farmers, no matter their age or circumstances.

---

* Thomas Jefferson, *The Papers of Thomas Jefferson, Volume 23: 1 January to 31 May 1792*, ed. Charles T. Cullen (Princeton, NJ: Princeton University Press, 1955), 438.

† "Indentured Servants in the U.S.," History Detectives Special Investigations, PBS, www.pbs.org/opb/historydetectives/feature/indentured-servants -in-the-us.

For that reason, after completing their indenture, many Brethren traveled with Mennonites, Moravians, and other Germans southward through Virginia's Great Valley, and continued to the Blue Ridge by traveling the Great Wagon Road and the Carolina Road. Thomas Jefferson's father, Peter, a surveyor as well as planter, was the first, along with his partner, Joshua Fry, to map the original route through the Virginia valley, referring to the road on the map alternately as the "Indian Road by Treaty of Lancaster," the "Waggon Road," or "The Great Road from the Yadkin River through Virginia to Philadelphia distant 455 Miles," as written on their map.* Thomas Jefferson passed northward on horseback along this route on his trips to the Continental Congress in Philadelphia. By the mid-1700s, a community of German Baptist Brethren had migrated through Big Lick (today's Roanoke) and traveled from there into today's Franklin County, where eventually both my parents were born, and where one of the largest contingents of Brethen continues to live today. Some of the Brethren went farther, eventually settling in the Winston-Salem area of North Carolina, which is still famous today for its Moravian community.

The Brethren named their first settlement in Franklin County "Germantown," incorporating it in 1765. They lived and farmed in a close-knit community so strong that the members continued to speak German for several generations after their arrival. Believing they should be "in the world, but not of it," they remained apart from American governance and creeds as much as feasible, with some even attempting to become conscientious objectors in the American Revolution. In 1782, these Franklin County Brethren, one of the few major German Baptist settlements south of the Mason-Dixon Line, joined in a brotherhood-wide statement declaring slavery to be against God's will and an anathema to their faith. The elders voted

---

* "Fry-Jefferson map of Virginia, 1751, showing the Great Wagon Road," Anchor: A North Carolina Online Resource, www.ncpedia.org/media/map /fry-jefferson-map.

that all Brethren should free any enslaved people they held, giving them money and clothing to start out on their own. My grandma Jamison's grandfather, Peter Eichenberg, the first male German Baptist ancestor in our family to enter Franklin County, was one of the early elders to sign a petition asking Confederate leaders for exemption from serving in the military during the Civil War.*

During my fieldwork among the Brethren of today, I found that many members continued to think of themselves as exiles in this world. Though devoted to their community of believers, and with many members still farming their own land that their ancestors procured, they have never come to believe they are rightful owners, or fully settled in place. Their home is not of this world, they say.

After living among so many former exiles in Guatemala, I came to understand that holding on to land as a farmer is nearly always an uncertain undertaking. Through my domestic research, I saw how the Maya's story relates to the Brethren's interpretation of continuing exile. Considering themselves sojourners in this world, the Old German Baptist Brethren identify as strangers traveling through the world without the certainty of settled and confident ownership of it. Their plain clothing, reminiscent of that of the Amish, and their separation from society are meant to identify them as belonging to God's Kingdom. Even Brethren farmers with hundreds of acres of land say they try to put their treasures in heaven, not on earth. By studying Grandma Jamison's people, I also learned how tenuous holds on places had helped the Brethren formulate a theology of marginality rather than possession. The Brethren gave me new words for what it means to be unsettled in a land of contradictions. I now understood even more about why I needed to return to my ancestors' stories. They had much to teach about farming and migration among living peoples today.

---

* Charles D. Thompson, Jr., *The Old German Baptist Brethren* (Urbana and Chicago, IL: University of Illinois Press, 2006), 32.

Clifford Thompson sharing a cup of coffee with his eldest grandson, the author. Photograph by Hope Shand.

Renewing | *1997, 2015*

*A*t the age of forty-one, having finished graduate school and with a son of my own, I felt lucky to be in a pickup beside my grandpa going somewhere we both wanted to go. How many times had he been at the wheel with me in the seat beside him? Now I was the one driving. I had gone to pick him up at his farm where he still lived with my aunt, helped him into my truck by lifting his arm at the elbow so he could slide into the seat on the passenger side. Two decades after we had first danced during my first year of college, we were heading up the winding mountain road, called Shooting Creek, to the Floyd Country Store, where we would get out on the dance floor with dozens of others and shuffle side by side one more time to local old-time string music. I had no clue that night would be our last opportunity. A man in his mid-eighties knows every dance can be his last. A man in his forties is only starting to get an inkling of that awareness.

In the darkness of that early-fall evening, and staring straight ahead into my headlights shining on the road, I decided I had to ask a question that had long been nagging me. Since Grandpa lived with my aunt now and he and I were rarely alone together, this was my chance. My question had to do with his personal finances, and, as everyone in the family knew, money was a subject he didn't talk about. Despite being uncomfortable with raising the topic, I needed to understand how a poor person from Endicott—a descendant of generations of tenants and poor farmers as far as we had any information about—could have made the jump to landownership as a young man.

I began by stating what I already knew. "I know you and Grandma bought a hundred and fifty acres and built a good house back in the 1930s," I said, "and you have told me a lot about your life in Endicott when you were growing up. But I still don't understand how you went from that life to buying a larger farm." I continued by recalling that he had mentioned on several occasions that he went to West Virginia as a teenager to make money. I knew he had not been a coal miner.

"I know you worked extra hard when you were a child in Endicott and you've told me about making a nickel washing dishes after lunch while everyone else rested. You saved every cent you made, and you even had to hide your savings from your siblings. You told me you bought your first car when you were a teenager. And you mentioned that you sometimes drove to West Virginia. But I still don't know how you got from Endicott to buying your farm?" I had all the pieces to the puzzle but one.

As we wound around the curves of Shooting Creek surrounded by the remnants of the farms of our ancestors—our conversation had to take place in Endicott—he revealed the rest of the story. In a quiet but confident tone that indicated it was time for me to know, he said, "I hauled bootleg liquor in my car to the coalfields." Then he continued with more details, as though he had been waiting to tell someone in the family all his life, and he probably had. He said his car had been shot at and even hit a few times as he drove with a caravan of liquor runners at top speed through Roanoke County and then over the Alleghenies, with the last car in the line weaving back and forth across the road to prevent the lawmen from heading off the pack. That was during the age before widespread police radio communication, so at the state line drivers were free to cross undeterred. They then delivered their loads to the miners living in dry company coal camps who were desperate for something to relieve their boredom and pain. It was a simple scheme dreamed up by entrepreneurs who took advantage of both Prohibition and the impoverished men (and women) living in a nearly cashless economy—those willing to drive their own cars for money, even if their cargo was illegal and even if it meant risking their lives. They hauled the homemade liquor to sites where other Appalachian people were living on starvation wages in cramped places with no access to land, cold water, homegrown corn, or relief. The drivers unloaded their five-gallon cans at some bootleg depot in a coal camp and then hightailed it back. The money made on the illegal deals mostly accrued to the "big wheels," the same ones who used a pyramid scheme to get Franklin County moonshine all the way to Philadelphia and New York and then pocketed the profits from every batch made, and every load hauled. Yet, even as a pawn in that plot, Grandpa had made enough money to make a down payment on his farm, and had lived all those years to tell about it. My gentle, teetotaler grandfather had kept quiet for nearly seventy years—not even my father knew that story. This was the missing piece about how my Thompson family made it out of poverty.

The picture of our family farm history changed instantly for me. Now I knew it was his peril—not the good fortune of some general American agrarianism—that led me to believe I, too, could be a farmer. The American Dream had not provided this start for us after all. Instead, my grandfather had found a way to landownership despite the strikes against him; not by the help of a government program but through ingenuity and risk-taking. This revelation suddenly gave me more insight into why, since childhood, I had been drawn to stories of hardship in agriculture, both the plights of small landowners and the landless. Is it possible that our hidden histories have a way of inspiring us to seek them out? I'll likely never know. But I do know this: Receiving this missing piece of Grandpa's story helped me link our family's tenure in agriculture to other widespread injustices in American landownership. Grandpa had to break the law to buy his land, and this reality gave me even greater empathy for people who continue to fight for their rights even while laboring as hidden "illegals" in our agricultural system—too many of them with no possibility of advancing into ownership—as well as for those who work on farms through their best years with no ownership loans in the offing. This realization gave me renewed sensitivity for any would-be farmers who work on organic or conventional farms today with no clear path to landownership. Now I know without a doubt just how desperate my ancestors—both those I knew personally and those long since deceased—had been to get a little piece of America. I had learned they were desperate enough centuries ago to leave family, go into debt as indentured laborers, and never return to their motherland; but now I had learned we were even willing to be shot at to get land. But you would have to meet Grandpa to understand how unlikely that scene was. No stereotypes about moonshiners and NASCAR drivers and hillbillies can come close to his story. He was the consummate gentleman, a just man, who became the impetus for my book about moonshine titled *Spirits of Just Men: Mountaineers, Liquor Bosses, and Lawmen in the Moonshine Capital of the World.*

I stood for all of them:
My ancestors whose voices continue to call to me.
Just women and men.
The rural poor and dispossessed.
Those who never owned land, and the ones who
    somehow came by it.
Those who worked under whip and in chains.
The foreclosed and the bankrupted,
Both those who left quietly,
And those pushed off their places in protest.
The people whose lives lie buried under soil, never
    having had their say,
And those for whom the myth of ownership
    never arrived.
The ones living and dying in refugee camps,
on reservations,
in food deserts,
in company towns after the companies have gone.

For those who have worked all their lives on
   farms never owning an acre.
For migrants and refugees working for starvation
   wages in U.S. food systems.
For families in sending communities south of the
   border who await their return.
For the idealistic young people who today are
   working for others,
But with no way to afford farms of their own.
For all the little people who, when added
   together, are not so little anymore.

"All of them" refers here to the legions whom I tried to hold close to my heart as I joined Hope and ninety others for nonviolent training at the AME Zion Church to prepare to be arrested in the summer of 2015. Reverend Dr. William Barber II and other leaders of the movement organized by the NAACP had started a series of weekly protests, coined "Moral Mondays," as an effort to take back the moral high ground from evangelicals who had exchanged their concern for the poor for political power. These protests were a call on elected leaders in North Carolina to do right by what the Bible calls the "least of these," the blessed poor who are—someday—to inherit the earth. Those poor and marginalized people had always borne the burden of our society's greed and exploitation, said Barber, the charismatic state director of the organization. He had become our prophet whose jeremiad was a response to a right-wing takeover of the state legislature. He had preached against their new laws that shut a half million people out of Medicare, reduced school funding in poor communities, and worsened environmental degradation. He included in his list of wrongs, as too few politicians had, how rural people were losing jobs and homes due to policies that served environmental polluters, hog integrators, and land grabbers. Deftly, he and the NAACP had added farm losses and other rural issues to their panoply of causes against which we stood demonstrating. And they had built a coalition of demonstrators from all over the state, not just the urban areas. Each week, the movement drew tens of thousands to the protests. By the end of the summer, nearly a thousand of us would be arrested for practicing civil disobedience—mostly singing, praying, and clapping—inside the North Carolina legislative building, or the people's house as some called it.

Friends of ours had joined the first wave. Their pictures were in the papers, their hands cinched behind their backs with white plastic cable ties. Three weeks later, Hope and I joined the fourth wave of arrestees. Given our job security and the fact that we had no criminal record, we knew we would face relatively low risks, especially in comparison with the working people whose jobs were on the line. "Government of the people, for the people, and by the people," we chanted in unison. We were worried about our very democracy being gutted by those who seemed to care only about padding the pockets of the rich while denying crucial services to the poor. Joining Reverend Barber on stage on more than one occasion, and adding inspiration for me, was Gary Grant, president of the Concerned Citizens of Tillery (CCT), with whom I had worked on the documentary film *We Shall Not Be Moved*. CCT's story began with African American sharecroppers receiving loans to buy land through FDR's Rural Resettlement Administration, FmHA's progressive predecessor. The film tells the hopeful story of their resettlement, but then continues to document FmHA's foreclosure on the farm belonging to Gary's parents and brother, Richard. Despite these setbacks, the film ends with the story of the CCT, a fighting group of senior citizens who refer to themselves as the "Open-Minded Seniors" and who continue to stage effective protests against land loss, corporate hog farms, voter disfranchisement, and other rural injustices. Standing on the stage for the Moral Mondays coalition that day, Gary spoke movingly for these causes of rural justice, as I had heard him do many times. His speech made me feel even more certain I was ready to go through with the arrest.

In preparation during the Sunday evening before, I spent time thinking about the meaning of justice in America. As I did so, I recalled Henry David Thoreau. By then I had learned more about his life and actions. I had learned, for example, that before moving to Walden, Thoreau and his family had worked with the Underground Railroad. Though I had no hint of these political leanings when I'd first tacked Thoreau's quotes to the walls of Grandpa's cabin, by 2015, I had read "Civil Disobedience" and knew how Thoreau had influenced, among others, Gandhi and then MLK, who had written that he read and reread the influential essay at Morehouse College. Again, I wrote out a Thoreau quote, but this time on a small, folded slip of paper that I put in my wallet. I told myself that if I began to waver as the officers approached with their handcuffs, I would pull out the quote and read it again, reminding myself why I had decided to go through with the act in the first place. The quote read: "If . . . the machine of government . . . be of such a nature that it requires you to be the agent of injustice to another, then, I say, break the law."

During the years Thoreau had been growing beans, contemplating simplicity, and living the life he had imagined, he also decided to take a stand against further slavery and imperialism advanced by the Mexican-American War and the subsequent annexation of Mexican territory. He served a night in jail for refusing to pay a poll tax, an act he engaged in specifically because of slavery and the seizure of Mexican land, including Texas, which was shortly thereafter turned into a slave state. Thoreau, in other words, did more than merely write about his beliefs. He acted on them. I had come to respect Thoreau when I was a teenager reading *Walden*, but he went so much further than I realized then. I had grown and changed, and I found him waiting to meet me again forty years later.

Our group of potential arrestees met at the St. Paul AME Church in Raleigh, where we prayed, sang, and held a press conference before walking two-by-two into the state legislative building. When we arrived, thousands more were already surrounding the building in support of our direct action. After hearing rousing speeches from the appointed speakers, we walked in a procession toward the door of the state senate. The crowd cheered as we walked by. When we reached the interior as a smaller group, we stood before an indoor fountain surrounded by plants and started singing in unison. Hundreds of others who supported our action filed onto the surrounding balcony. Over ninety of us clasped hands, formed two solid lines in front of the senate chamber, and continued singing and praying.

Then came the warning from the police chief who shouted into a megaphone, cautioning that those who did not leave immediately would be taken to jail. We already knew from our training that admonition would be coming. We stood our ground. We had been taught nonviolent resistance, so our task was to remain steadfast but also to allow ourselves to be taken peacefully by the State Capitol Police. Within a few minutes, the officers began to bind our hands and escort us out, and we cooperated. They began with the people to my right. Among the first few to be taken were a woman in a wheelchair and several other elderly women and men, both Black and white, including one person in a clerical collar, who needed assistance to walk. I found myself feeling a little sorry for the police as I watched them take away members of the clergy and others who appeared to be the least threatening group imaginable. Yet, I also knew that though the protestors might have been weak in body, their witness was stronger than any brute force in the world. In reality, most of us knew little else we could do to try to stem the tide of greed, fear, and hatred that seemed to be overtaking our heretofore moderate state. So we took a stand, even if our individual actions seemed minuscule in the face of such powerful forces backed by millions of dollars of lobbyist money.

When those forces came for Hope and me, suddenly the struggle seemed very personal. I watched to make sure she was unharmed, as if I could have done anything if she was hurt, and then I was cuffed and taken by the elbow and walked out, too. As we were led away, the entire group sang, "This little light of mine, I'm going to let it shine." The officers escorted small groups of us onto an elevator that took us one floor down to a holding area. From there, when they had completed the arrests, they would transfer us to awaiting buses and drive to the county jail for fingerprinting and booking.

As we joined the rest in the holding area with our hands cinched tight, I felt a strong sense of kinship among us that I hadn't felt before. I thought of the old hymn "Paul and Silas Bound in Jail All Night Long," a song about their spiritual uplift while in prison. After all of us were taken downstairs, the police escorted us outside to the cheers of hundreds of supporters on the street. As we made our way on the bus toward the Wake County jail, we started singing again, this time the old chorus written by members of the Southern Tenant Farmers' Union: "Ain't gonna let nobody turn me round, turn me round, turn me round. Ain't gonna let nobody turn me round. Gonna keep on walking, keep on talking, marching into freedom's land." Though I had sung the words before, I had never felt their meaning as I did then. No church service I'd ever been part of had felt that deep, either.

Even as the plastic ties dug into my wrists and the seats felt harder by the minute, I began to realize that this bus was my church and the bus seats, the pews. The people surrounding me were my tribe, my kin united in action on behalf of others. Though we were different from one another—we were of many faiths, all ages, and diverse races and genders—we understood that we were united in a belief in justice that says that until everyone is given safe harbor and enjoys liberty and the pursuit of happiness within a society, none can be truly free. Knowing we had gotten nowhere close to that kind of justice in our state, many of us felt we were exactly where we needed to be. Because our government had done harm to others, we had broken the law. We had followed Thoreau's example of deepest citizenship.

On the police bus that day, I felt as much at home as any sojourner can feel anywhere. My work for justice seemed to cohere in this act of civil disobedience. I thought of my arrest as counting for those I carried with me: the legions of rural people who had suffered losses on both sides of the US-Mexico border and elsewhere. I imagined all of them standing with me that day, side by side, even as the officers fingerprinted me alone.

Doug Wallin's seedbed. Photograph by Rob Amberg.

Covering

*C*overing—the simple process of pushing soil over seeds—is one
of the most hopeful acts humans can engage in. Yet even as
this word appears on my screen, it brings to mind the forty-three
Ayotzinapa students of the Rural Teachers' College who were killed
in Iguala, Guerrero, Mexico, in 2014. The students had been studying to teach in rural elementary schools in Guerrero. Then, they
participated in a protest against discriminatory hiring practices for
teachers, and now they are dead.

In fighting to bring their children's murderers to justice, the
families and their supporters invoked the aphorism attributed to
Greek poet Dinos Christianopoulos: "They tried to bury us, but
they did not know we were seeds." The families meant that, despite
the atrocity, the justice and truth they stand for, like seeds buried
beneath the ground, will sprout from the soil into the light, and
bring change. Vowing to never forget the forty-three, the families
say they will continue to echo the voices of their silenced young
leaders, and indeed they have done so.

I met and talked with some of the family members of the murdered students when they came through Durham, North Carolina
in March 2015, on their way to seek support from the US government in Washington, DC. When I heard them speak, I recognized
immediately that their bravery and fighting spirit belonged to people
of the land. Their willingness to risk their lives for justice was of the
same resolve that I had witnessed often among the rural poor in
Latin America and in the United States amid other struggles. Their

use of the metaphor of seeds in Ayotzinapa succinctly captured the spirit I have tried to tap into when working for change in farming and in rural life in general—a spirit of hope that springs from agricultural regeneration.

But I must admit that my positivity about rural America has taken a beating recently, especially since 2016. In my lowest moments, I have wondered whether rural America still possesses a fighting spirit and whether our farm communities will be able to emerge from our failures and grow toward the justice and inclusion so many have worked for over the generations. Sometimes I have had to ask, do we in America still have a spirit of hope ready to sprout from our fallow ground? If they try to bury us, are we seeds?

We have heard ad infinitum that the result of the 2016 presidential election was due to rural Americans revolting at the voting booth. We have also heard incessantly that the kind of populism "rural Americans" espoused tied their hopes for a renewed rural economy to the vilification of Mexican immigrants, Blacks, Muslims, and seemingly just about anybody other than straight whites. Their nostalgia for America's past sounded more like xenophobia than hope, more like spraying poisons than planting seeds for a new season. As these American "rural" voters helped usher in a new administration, it seemed fear rather than freedom had won the day, that Americans had begun believing that equality and participatory democracy are the problem rather than cherished ideals, that welcoming immigrants in a nation built by immigrants works against us, and that even taking care of the environment would somehow make America less powerful. Had a wall at our southern border really become for them a more apt symbol of our country than the torch held high by the Statue of Liberty? I worried that America was losing its identity as the home of the brave and free, and was fast becoming a bastion of the embittered and afraid who are willing to sell their very souls for personal and, by extension, corporate gain at the expense of the powerless.

Yet, a part of me also knows this is not the whole story. As in any society, there has always existed racism and a fear of difference in the United States. There have always been scapegoats. Yet thankfully there have also always been people in rural America who reject these tendencies. I believe this because I came of age in a place where rural Americans cared about neighbors, visited the shut-ins, rebuilt others' burned barns, gave food to the needy, and showed up for each other when flood and fire struck. Rural people, including rural African Americans, indigenous peoples, Latinx people, and others, have embraced me, despite our different backgrounds and my naïveté. As a community organizer, I witnessed the spirit that some call the spirit of the Good Samaritan, which shows that love can overcome its enemies, fear and indifference. Today, the central question of that parable remains, even as it was written two thousand years ago: "Who is my neighbor?"

Are there rural Americans who will embrace neighbors who do not look like them, go beyond tribalism and fear, and welcome diverse allies in the struggle for common goals? Will rural whites come to see that their future is tied to racial, environmental, and economic justice for all? I believe the answers to these questions will determine whether our national drive to form a "more perfect union" can survive. Everything America stands for is riding on this.

For those who believe in the regeneration of seeds, much work lies ahead of us. In divided families and communities, we need people who are willing to listen to others, even when we may want to turn our backs and condemn. We also need those who will push back against intolerance. We need people who will join the oppressed in their fight for justice, knowing change will never come on its own, and that inequality will only worsen if we remain idle.

Believing in justice also means asking others with whom we may disagree to "please explain," and to be willing to listen through misunderstandings. Successful communities cannot begin with condemnation or the dismissal of others. As hard as it may be, we must seek to understand the real pain in rural America that breeds the social cancers of racism and hatred of difference. I know from direct experience that the loss of good jobs is real, that coal communities and small manufacturing towns have suffered great harm, that farm communities have been battered beyond recognition, and that these wounds have made people turn against others in misguided back-lashes. When threatened, people can lash out and vilify others, and we know from many periods of history that the instinct to blame is the root of much tyranny in the world and that the powerful can use divisions to further amass power for themselves. To counteract such tendencies, we must seek to understand the roots of rural discontent. Leaders in communities must be courageous and stand against bigotry, and they must also listen for the pain, never in order to foment or use to their gain the hate that brews when people feel wronged, but to address the real losses that make citizens turn to rash judgments. Only when suffering people hear their worst fears repeated back to them in constructive ways can we hope for reconciliation and to find common ground.

The great challenge before us, whether in Appalachia, the rural South, or anyplace in the world, is to plant seeds of hope and change in soil that has been soured by anger and division. Transformation of this sort always begins with looking for an opening. To find one, we need active understanding, followed by constructive education and development of new opportunities. We need rural organizers who will stay for the long haul, believing in rural people, and believing that education and proper access to funding can help people solve their own problems. Above all, we must seek ways for people to hear one another across dividing lines.

I came from ancestors who were once marginalized people who experienced only glimmers of change. But from their descendants, I know that national efforts to empower those left out made my education possible, and that public investment led ultimately to my work for change within rural communities. Knowing this, I could never claim I did anything completely on my own. This assures me that others can benefit from public investment, too.

I know from experience that rebuilding of rural communities must include making federal agricultural credit available to young people. There is a resurgence of interest in local farming and we know that many are ready to volunteer on farms. How we respond to this new upsurge of interest and how we help transform these willing workers from glorified sharecroppers into farm owners is a key subject that will influence the very future of rural democracy in this nation. Will we provide grants and loans to foster this entrepreneurial spirit among our nation's new farmers, including youths of color, who want to do the hard work of farming in the coming era of climate change? Providing them with means to landownership and food production is essential for reversing negative trends that have been decades in the making. Reducing environmental protections and unleashing corporate farming, coal mining, and other extractive industries—all strategies espoused by those who want to capitalize negatively on rural discontent—may bring a brief but fleeting boost to a few incomes in the short run. But abandoning protections cannot represent any hope for our collective future in the long run. Lashing out against other countries does no long-term good, either.

Our hope lies in embracing rural places as our homes, and treating them as beloved gardens we tend and are inspired by. These places can be where we raise children and take care of the elderly—home places are where we love neighbors as ourselves, not just those we choose, but, as Wendell Berry has said, the neighbors we have. Home is where we begin and end, and where we plant our seeds for the next generation. We all know there is much fallow ground waiting to be loved, and thankfully we still have many waiting to try. These hopeful people are also humanity's seeds waiting to sprout and grow. Let us nurture them with care.

ACKNOWLEDGMENTS

*R*eaders will recognize that this entire book is one grand acknowledgment of those who have influenced and assisted me in innumerable ways: teachers, mentors, family members, and organizations run by agents of change. Though I have not arrived at any resting point, am still seeking answers to questions long in the making, and am still striving to make sense of the frayed and loose strands of my life, I pause to thank those who have helped me make it this far, the named in this book along with the unnamed who contributed their work and wisdom to push me toward believing in justice and the light of freedom for all. I strive to inherit and live up to your dreams. I would have gotten nowhere without you.

To my teachers and mentors, thank you for your sacrifice, for believing, sometimes beyond visible evidence, that breakthroughs are possible. Among them: D. B. Waddle, Gerald Blankenship, David Henry, Ethel Caywood, Doug Boyce, Fred Kellogg, Steve Fisher, Doris Betts, Robert Kirkpatrick, Ruel Tyson, Jim Peacock, Della Pollock, Bill Peck, Dottie Holland, Evelyn Mattern, Jeff Boyer, Daniel Patterson, Will Campbell, Gail Phares, Collins Kilburn, Joe Mann, Betty Bailey, Si Kahn, Ken Dawson, Mona Lee Brock, and countless others. Thanks also to my students, whom I always deem as teachers as well as learners.

To my colleagues and friends, thank you for believing in and encouraging me: Tom Rankin, Iris Tillman Hill, Courtney Reid-Eaton, the Center for Documentary Studies, Laurie Patton, Malinda Maynor Lowery, Louise and Waltz Maynor, Melinda Wiggins, Ray Gavins, Cynthia Hill, Keny Murillo, Graham Harvey, Michelle Lanier, Brian Giemsa, Mike Wiley, Allan Gurganus, Bob Thompson, Randall Kenan, Norman Wirzba, Jed Purdy, Lee Smith, Marcie and Bill Ferris, Melinda Wiggins and Student Action with Farmworkers, Carolyn Mugar, Jennifer Fahy, Farm Aid, Sharon Hicks, John Chasteen, Mark Simpson-Vos, Harlan Campbell, Tim

Tyson, David Cecelski, Adriane Lentz-Smith, Alice Gerrard, Chris Potter, Michael Davey, Cornelio Campos, Natalie Hartman, Bruce Martin, Gary Grant, Orin Starn, Lee Baker, members of Duke's Department of Cultural Anthropology, Vaughan Webb, Roddy Moore, the Blue Ridge Institute at Ferrum College, Rob Vaughan, Jeanne Siler, David Bearinger and Virginia Humanities, Witness for Peace, The Gentlemen's Book and Bottle Club, Mark Davidson and the Church of the Rec, and the countless others whose work for justice and peace has inspired me.

To my parents and grandparents, sister and brother, aunts, uncles, and cousins, along with all of those ancestors whose blood runs through you: You are my bedrock. To our son Marshall who upon birth was already filled with questions and new lessons: Thank you for never giving up. To my wife, Hope, thank you for believing and reading and editing and always giving beyond measure. You send me.

Thank you, Rob Amberg, for your photographs and inspiration, and for accompanying me on many journeys over land and ideas. Thank you, Bonnie Campbell, for helping me select and edit the photographs and for helping me understand the art of books. Thanks to Chris Liu-Beers for your web design work.

Thank you to our friend and mentor, Gary Nabhan, for putting me in touch with Chelsea Green Publishing, specifically with acquisitions editor Ben Watson. Special thanks to Michael Metivier for your close editing and encouragement, and to the many others at the press whose efforts made this book possible.

Thanks to life and love and the universe of possibilities. Thanks to all who seek justice, love mercy, and reach across borders. Thanks to all the seeds I have held and covered with soil, believing in another season's harvest, and to those human seeds whose lives have been covered only to resurrect as irrepressible hope. Thanks to my readers. With your help, may this book do some good in the world.

INDEX

Note: Page numbers in *italics* refer to photographs; page numbers followed by *n* refer to footnotes.

African Americans
    in civil rights movement, 33–34, 124
    at Graham Center, 116, 117
    at Koinonia Farm, 96–99
    landownership of, 97, 98, 118, 123–24,
      140, 143, 185–87
    loan discrimination affecting, 4, 119,
      130–32, 137–38, 141, 186–87
    loan foreclosures affecting, 138, 208
    migration to northern cities, 94, 123
    at North Carolina A & T State
      University, 121–24
    RAF hotline calls from, 130, 137
    in RAF multiracial coalition, 130–32
    as sharecroppers, 93
    in Southern Tenant Farmers' Union, 137
    in United Farmers Organization, 137–41
agrarian ideal of Jefferson, 108, 109, 110, 111
agribusiness, 35, 39, 168–73
    confined animal feeding in, 170
    and Future Farmers of America, 43–44
    globalization of, 179
    government encouragement of, 35, 53,
      96, 108, 118, 126, 146
    labor practices in, 169
    and loss of rural work, 93–94
    and loss of small family farms, 25, 26, 27,
      108, 171
    in North Carolina, 163
    organic growers against, 50
    organic produce in, 168–69
    university research for, 119, 122, 171
Agricultural Adjustment Act, 96
agricultural justice, 111
Agricultural Marketing Act, 96
agrochemicals, 35. *See also* pesticides

Alcott, Bronson, 61
All God's Dangers: The Life of Nate Shaw
    (Rosengarten), 93, 116
alternative farming movement, 107, 109,
    112
American Agriculture Movement, 27, 126
    Tractorcade of, 26–27, 126, 139
American Dream, 94, 98, 111, 187, 205
American Farm Crisis, 6, 26–27, 170
Americus GA
    food shortage in, 91, 92
    fresh vegetables distributed in, 91–93
    Koinonia Farm in, 89–99
    poverty in, 92, 93
Ammons, George, 137
Anderson, Elizabeth, 148–49, 158
Anson County NC, Graham Center in,
    115–19
Appalachia
    Emory & Henry studies on, 84–86
    Foxfire books on culture of, 63
    identification with, 86
    landownership study in, 86
    stereotypes on, 84–85
Appalachian Studies Association, 84
Armstrong, Neil, 39
Atkins VA
    adolescence of CDT in, 37–40, 44–45,
      46
    Robinette place in, 37–38, *39*
    Thompson family moving to, 34
auctions
    farm, *42*
    livestock, 21–23, *80*, 183
Ayotzinapa students, protest and murder
    of, 213–14